D0374800

RENEWALS 458-4574

Religious Nuts, Political Fanatics

WITHDRAWN

UTSA Libraries

Religious Nuts, Political Fanatics

U2 in Theological Perspective

Robert Vagacs

Cascade Books

A division of *Wipf & Stock Publishers*

199 West 8th Avenue, Suite 3 • Eugene OR 97401

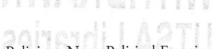

Religious Nuts, Political Fanatics
U2 in Theological Perspective

Copyright © 2005 Robert Vagacs. All rights reserved. Except for brief quotations in critical publications or reviews, no part of this book may be reproduced in any manner without prior written permission from the publisher. Write: Permissions, Wipf & Stock, 199 W. 8th Ave., Eugene, OR 97401.

ISBN: 1-59752-336-4

Cataloging information:

Vagacs, Robert
     Religious nuts, political fanatics : U2 in theological perspective / by Robert Vagacs.

        p.; cm.
        1. U2 (Musical group). 2. Culture—Study and teaching. 3. Rock musicians—Ireland. 4. Music—20th century—History and criticism. 5. Music—21st century—History and criticism I. Title.

     ISBN 1-59752-336-4

     ML421.U2 V34 2005

Excerpts from *Prophetic Imagination* by Walter Brueggemann © 2001 Fortress Press, *Finally Comes the Poet* by Walter Brueggemann © 1989 Fortress Press, and *The Psalms and the Life of Faith* by Walter Brueggemann © 1995 Fortress Press. Used by permission.

Excerpts from *Hope Against Hope: Christian Eschatology at the Turn of the Millennium* by Richard Bauckham and Trevor Hart, © 1999 Wm. B. Eerdmans Publishing Co., Grand Rapids, Michigan. Used by permission.

Library
University of Texas
at San Antonio

Manufactured in the U.S.A.

For my sister Susan, and my father Attila,

"You're packing a suitcase for a place none of us has been / A place that has to be believed to be seen."

What we think of as our destination,

Is really another point of departure.

Our homecoming heralds a new adventure.
See you when I get home.

Contents

Acknowledgements

U2's first North American leg of its Vertigo Tour culminated in Boston, Massachusetts. It was Tuesday night, and along with my friends Mike, Jeff, and Mike, I just enjoyed the spectacle with thousands of fans at the Fleet Center. Section 305, Row 8, Seat 4. A special hello to my newfound friends from Halifax. You made the show that much more fun. I did a little people watching that evening and noticed something that reminded me of U2's previous tour, the Elevation Tour. People of all ages, races, and social strata were in attendance. The fan reviews from u2.com reflect this as well. I met fans from as far away as Vermont, London, and La Paz, Bolivia. They prompt me to ask what is it exactly about U2's music that captivates people from such a diverse demographic, not to mention geographic, diversity? Is it their consistency, or their cohesiveness as a band? Is it their commitment to the music and each other? Is it U2's concern and involvement with social justice issues? Perhaps it's simply the fact that they generate great music.

So what is the draw? In Anton Corbijn's latest book, *U2 & i*, Michael Stipe, lead singer of R.E.M., confesses, "I'm pretty sure that neither Anton, Bono, Edge, Larry, nor Adam have any idea of the enormous impact that they have had on me, in my life, challenging and prompting me either in person or through their work. It is a rich gift to offer to anyone, the ability to inspire, and for me that gift has not gone unnoticed."[1] I believe people gravitate to the band because indeed, U2 does inspire. U2 creates and offers a message of hope. In this fragmented, post-September 11 world of isolation and angst, hope can often be difficult to come by. When it does appear, however, it is recognized as fresh and inspiring, and it is latched onto. This is the appeal of U2; especially of U2 performing their songs live. As Bono noted in their Elevation Tour Book, "U2 on its own is a very interesting group and all, but U2 with its audience is a *culture* . . . If you stop meeting your audience you start mistrusting them and they you. And you cease being a cultural entity, just a musical one." Having firsthand knowledge of seeing U2 perform, I can attest to the truth of that statement. U2 has a way of not only transforming a cavernous arena into an intimate living room, but of conveying their message of hope right into the listeners' hearts. This is why people have traveled from all over to see U2 perform. This is why three of my friends and I made the rainy trek from Toronto to Boston. We all long for a message of hope; a message that reminds us there is something greater beyond ourselves; a message that tells us with God and humanity partnering together, great and wonderful things can be achieved. From my vantage point, up in section 305, this is the captivating magnetism of the twenty-five-year-old phenomenon called U2.

For the past two decades, U2's music and message have resonated with my own life. Larry Mullen Jr. once described the U2 movie and album *Rattle and Hum* as a musical journey. I think it fair to say that the journey U2 embarked on twenty-five years ago is more than a musical one. It is a biblical journey. It is a theological journey. This book is written from the perspective of a passenger along on that journey, noting observations along the way.

By no means, though, have I written this alone. I am indebted to the following passengers for their influence and encouragement. Special thanks are due to my long lost friend, Jason Santerre, who first introduced me to the Irish lads by giving me my first ever U2 cassette, *October*. On occasion, I still find myself humming "Gloria," "I Threw A Brick Through A Window," and "Tomorrow."

---

[1] Anton Corbijn, *U2&i* (Verona: Schirmer/Mosel, 2005) 33.

Acknowledgments

I am grateful for my mentors, John Stephenson and Brian Walsh, who have shown me that cultural studies, especially popular culture, have a place in the Church and can facilitate the message of the Gospel. I will always remember walking down the hall of a conservative bible college in Peterborough, Ontario, hearing "When Love Comes to Town" blasting out of John's soteriology class. I would eavesdrop, as John would explain what this song had to say about the crucifixion of Jesus Christ.

Thanks especially to the Wycliffe College community in Toronto for fostering an excellent learning environment, and to Brian Walsh for his acceptance of this work in its original form as a thesis (for the Master of Theological Studies program) titled, "The Poet's Voice in Postmodern Culture: Heard through the Music of U2." Your ongoing support of this project has been invaluable. I am indebted to your critical eye, intuitive mind, and kind spirit.

Special thanks also to K. C. Hanson, David Root, and Halden Doerge at Cascade Books for taking the time to review drafts and offer key comments. I am grateful for my most excellent publisher Jim Tedrick. Your support and assistance has been nothing short of outstanding.

Lastly, thank you Nicole. Thank you for your patience and love. Thank you for listening to my ramblings. Thank you for being a U2 fan! It has made this endeavor so much more enjoyable. It is a great joy and privilege to share the journey with you.

To the boys out there, who play rock and roll, thanks Bono, Adam, Larry, and Edge. Your music offers hope to an otherwise hurting and broken world. Keep dreaming out loud. Keep stopping the traffic.

Foreword

"I'm at a place called Vertigo." The words were penned by Bono and performed by U2, but this evening they were spoken by Henry as we walked down the hall of the Critical Care Unit of the Hospital for Sick Children in Toronto. At the end of that hall, Henry's wife Sarah was keeping vigil at the side of their daughter Hannah, now on life support, after spending most of her five months of life in this hospital.

And U2 was in town.

So where *was* my friend Henry? "I'm at a place called Vertigo." This may not be Club Vertigo. And it certainly wasn't a place that could afford the luxury of postmodern anomie and irony. But it was a place called Vertigo. How do you keep your bearings, how do you maintain orientation, how do you even know how you feel, when you've been with your daughter struggling for life this long?

In discussion with Michka Assayas, Bono once said that "the world demands to be described, and so, painters, poets, journalists, pornographers, and sitcom writers, by accident or by design, are just following orders, whether from high or low, to describe the world they're in."[1] But what about the world of Hannah, Sarah, and Henry? What

---

[1] *Bono in Conversation with Michka Assayas* (New York: Riverhead Books / Penguin, 2005) 26.

about my world as their friend, as someone who also loved baby Hannah? This world needs describing, yes; but more importantly, this world needs healing and hope.

These were not academic questions that week in September, 2005. You see, U2 was in town. And we all had tickets. Can you go to a U2 concert while Hannah is just blocks away in the critical care unit? Does that make any sense at all?

The initial answer was no. No, it didn't make sense to go to a concert this week. So we all started to make arrangements to sell our tickets. Henry and Sarah could not leave Hannah's side even for fifteen minutes, let alone a whole evening. And my wife, Sylvia, and I couldn't imagine enjoying a U2 show while things were so precarious with Hannah.

But two conversations changed our minds. One of my students took me aside after class and encouraged me to go to the concert. "This could be the most healing thing you can do all week," he suggested. And then another friend said, "good liturgy doesn't come to town very often. The least you can do is be there."

And so Sylvia and I went to hear U2 while our beloved Hannah was on life support just up the road. Could this rock band minister to us while we were accompanying Henry and Sarah in the shadow of the valley of death? Dare we even hope for such a thing from a rock concert? From the first song to the last, the answer was clearly yes.

So much of U2's music is created in the face of, and in response to, death. The concert opened with "City of Blinding Lights"—a song written in response to the events of 9/11 in New York City, yet rich enough to address a very different tragedy that we were facing that night. "Oh you look so beautiful tonight," Bono sings, and I'm thinking of that beautiful little girl in her hospital bed. "Oh you look so beautiful tonight," and I'm thinking about the tenderness of my friends holding their daughter. "And I miss you when you're not around," Bono sings to the lost souls of the Twin Towers, and to his father, and to the children who have disappeared in Chile and other places of oppression. And I hear those words coming to a place deep within myself as I have longed to have Hannah, Sarah, and Henry at home with us where they belong.

We are only one song into the concert, and I know that I'm in the right place.

Larry counts out four beats on his drum sticks, the Edge adds a percussive two measures on his guitar, Bono shouts out, "Unos dos tres catorce!" and the stage becomes a whirl of dizzying, swirling color, and the band is off to a place called Vertigo. Is this where I want to be? I just came from Vertigo, do I really want to follow U2 deeper into that place? And the answer is again yes. I didn't come to this concert to escape my grief, my fear, my vertigo. I came here knowing that U2 would meet me there, enter into the grief, describe this world and offer, in the very description, a word of hope. Yes this is a dangerous place, full of temptation, "it's everything I wish I didn't know." But even in this place, Bono sings, "I can feel your love teaching me how / Your love is teaching me how, how to kneel . . . " The place of vertigo is transposed into a place of prayer. And now we know that this concert is a place of worship, a call to prayer.

But what should we pray? What words do we find in such a situation? In the next song, the band launched into a toned-down version of "Elevation," and during the middle eight, Bono gives us the words to pray: "Love, lift me out of these blues / Won't you tell me something new / I believe in you." Bono the psalmist: Bono who won't avert his gaze from the blues, who won't countenance any cheap escape, but who will pray for something new because the same old shit just won't cut it anymore.

Within a few minutes, it is clear that Hannah is somehow on U2's radar screen. Bono introduces "Miracle Drug" by dedicating it to the folks who work so hard at the local children's hospital. That's Hannah's nursing staff he's talking about! And again, the band brings us back to prayer—"God I need your help tonight." Yes, that's why we are here. Not looking to U2 for salvation, but allowing the band to bear witness, allowing this "scribbling, cigar-smoking, wine-drinking, Bible-reading band man" to "make the light brighter," to illuminate the darkness we were facing.[2]

From song to song it seemed that the light did get just a little brighter. There were moments of immediate recognition. "Sometimes you can't make it on your own"—well, of course not. But "I don't know if I can take it / I'm not easy on my knees." As the band sang "Love and Peace or Else," the powerful political message was transformed into a deeply personal statement. "I need some release, release, release" was sung for all of us who have been hanging on a thread with baby Hannah. And when Bono sang, "As you

---

[2] Ibid., 43, 86.

enter this life / I pray you depart / With a wrinkled face / And a brand new heart," the tears began to flow. Hannah no longer has the wrinkled face of a newborn, and there is nothing wrong with the heart of this little one.

"I was born a child of grace," sings Bono in "All Because of You." "Child of grace." That's what *Hannah* means! I didn't come to this concert to get away from this little girl, and there seems to be nothing in the concert that will allow me to escape her precarious reality.

Rich liturgy—that's what a U2 concert is all about. Describing the world, opening the heart to grief as a doorway to hope. Prayer. The concert began with prayer, and ended with prayer. "Yahweh, Yahweh / Always pain before a child is born. Yahweh, Yahweh / Tell me now / Why the dark before the dawn?" Prayer and pain. Faith and longing questions. Deep darkness, longing for the dawn.

And then the last song: "I waited patiently for the Lord / He inclined and heard my cry / He brought me out of the pit / Out of the mire and clay." We are back with Bono in the Psalms. And somehow, in the midst of this concert, with Hannah's hospital room never far from my mind, I have a quiet confidence that my cry has been heard. But I still join my voice with thousands of others in the hall, "How long to sing this song / How long to sing this song?" To use the words of the prophet Isaiah, how long must we hear the cry of distress? How many more children must be born for calamity? Or, back to U2, how long until we can sing, "Then will there be no time for sorrow / Then will there be no time for pain / Then will there be no time for sorrow / Then will there be no time for shame" ("Playboy Mansion")?

In grief and sadness, in a state of vertigo, I went to a concert with some "religious nuts" and "political fanatics." I went to a rock concert by one of the biggest bands in the world expecting a liturgical experience that would be healing. Before going, my friend Rob Vagacs assured me that I would not be disappointed. He was right. And he should know. Not only has Rob been to more U2 concerts than I could count, and not only has he listened deeply to every U2 song ever released, and read pretty much everything ever written about them, he has also taken the pulse of this band, discerned the Spirit that leads them, and opened up the rich theological significance of the pop culture phenomenon known as U2.

U2 in theological perspective?—of course. What other perspective could anyone expect? Granted, many, if not most, of the folks in that concert hall didn't know that "40" is rooted in the Psalm 40, with an insertion of the "how long" of various psalms of lament. Granted, many of my fellow concert goers didn't pick up on the fact that Bono was praying in so many of his songs. Granted, images like a "dove with a leaf in her mouth" do not immediately remind a post-Christendom crowd of the story of Noah. Granted, folks don't necessarily know that "I and I in the sky" is a reference to God, or that the "you" in "All because of you, I am" is the Creator of all. But that doesn't matter because the prayers are there in the songs, and the lyrics literally drip with biblical allusion wherever you look.

This book takes the time to look. Vagacs isn't imposing a theological agenda on a secular band. Rather, he is taking up the theological invitation, indeed the theological challenge, inherent in the artistic vision of U2. This book isn't so much a theological exposition of the meaning of U2's lyrics as it is an entering into a conversation with the band because there are important matters that need to be discussed, places of darkness that need some light. U2 initiated this conversation; Vagacs has simply decided to enter in. And he invites us along for the ride.

Reacting against any cheap grace and junk-food religion, any easy escape from the burden, complexity, and grief of life, Bono once said that, "the true life of a believer is one of a longer, more hazardous or uphill pilgrimage . . . where you uncover slowly the sort of illumination for your next step."[3] The frenetic energy and the bright lights of the concert hall notwithstanding, the illumination is always slower, longer, and more hazardous. This is an uphill pilgrimage that we are on. But there is light for our path. Some of that light shines through the music and lyrics of U2.

Rob Vagacs does not come to worship at the shrine of U2. That would be a blasphemy to his own faith and a terrible disservice to the band. Rather, this book opens our eyes to light that is shining in the midst of the darkness of a postmodern world. U2 is not the light of the world. Jesus is. Rob Vagacs joins U2 in following that light, helps that light to shine brighter through his theological engagement with their music, and invites us to walk in that light.

—Brian Walsh
University of Toronto

---

[3] Ibid., 207.

Preface

You may be a diehard U2 fan, having taken in countless concerts, or a new fan, loving the band's latest albums. You may also be a student of theology, curious about what a rock and roll band has to do with God. The title of "Religious Nuts, Political Fanatics" stems from U2's song "New York."[1] I thought it appropriate due to the nature of this work, for this book is in fact about the religiously influenced, and politically charged music of U2.

Whether you find yourself to be a U2 fan, a theologian, both, or neither, I thought it would be helpful to offer a short glossary of terms at the beginning of the book, rather than at the end. Keep an eye out for the footnotes as well. After each cited song lyric, I have included a recommended listening note. I believe that U2's lyrics need to be listened to as well as read. This will allow you, the reader, to enhance your reading experience by making it interactive, thus gaining the most from this book. All of the music cited should be available at a local library, retailer, or downloadable from *iTunes* or another reputable online store.

In its original drafts, this book quoted U2 songs in their entirety to better contextualize the subject matter. At the time of publication, however,

---

[1] "New York," from the album *All That You Can't Leave Behind.* © 2000 Universal International Music BV.

I had not yet received permission from Universal Music, or from Principal Management to cite U2's songs in their entirety. Therefore only brief phrases and lines from songs are permitted to be used. As an alternative, I invite the reader to visit either U2's official website at u2.com, or an excellent fansite @u2.com for an exhaustive catalogue of U2's lyrics.

The following is a brief list of definitions that I trust will serve as an aid to understanding this work.

U2: U2 is an Irish rock band comprised of four band members: Bono (vocals), Adam Clayton (bassist), Larry Mullen Jr. (drummer), and The Edge (guitarist). They are by now the most viable and enduring rock band around—a cultural tour de force. For a better understanding of the band, kindly refer to the sources listed at the end of this book.

Theology: Christian theology can be described as "ongoing and is best characterized by the metaphor of pilgrimage. Christian theology is pilgrim theology."[2] In simpler terms, theology is humanity's ongoing discussion about God. If you find yourself having a conversation about whether or not God exists, you are having a theological conversation. If you ever think about the beauty of this universe and how it came to be, or the hostility that can be allowed to exist in such a beautiful place, you are thinking a theological thought. Be warned—by listening to a U2 song, theological thought and discussion could very well occur. [3]

Eschatology: This pertains to the final hope of every Christian. It is "the medium of Christian faith as such, the key in which everything is set, the glow that suffuses everything here in the dawn of an expected new day."[4] Put another way:

---

[2] Stanley J. Grenz and John R. Franke, *Beyond Foundationalism: Shaping Theology In A Postmodern Context* (Louisville: WJK Press, 2001) 17.
[3] For an excellent primer on theology, specifically Christian theology, see Daniel L. Migliore, *Faith Seeking Understanding: An Introduction to Christian Theology* (Grand Rapids: Eerdmans, 1991).
[4] Jürgen Moltmann, *Theology of Hope. On the Ground and Implications of a Christian Eschatology,* transl. J. Leitch (London: SCM Press, 1967) 15–16.

Preface

Christians hope in the final victory of the creative, self-expending, community-forming love of the triune God. Hence they hope in the triumph of the love of God over all hate, of the justice of God over all injustice, of God's freedom over all bondage, of community with God over all separation, of life with God over the power of death. Yet this hope becomes indistinguishable from cheap optimism if it fails to recognize and to share the present agony of the world.[5]

Eschatology is discussed mainly in chapter 3. However, there is an eschatological thread woven throughout this book.

Yahweh: Appearing over 6000 times in the Old Testament, this is the Hebrew name of God. It is believed that this is the name God revealed to Moses through the burning bush. According to scholars, it is the closest we have come to its pronunciation. When coming across it in this book, it can be used interchangeably for God or the LORD GOD.

Postmodernism: In the effort of trying to offer a succinct definition of postmodernism, I have come to the realization that every author has a slightly different interpretation of postmodernism. How fitting, since postmodernism is about, or at least in part about creating new meaning, and the fluidity of meaning. Try "Googling" *postmodernism* or search it through amazon.com and witness for yourself the dizzying amount of information. Grenz and Franke admit that postmodernism is notoriously difficult to pin down. Paul Lakeland notes that there are "probably a thousand different self-appointed commentators on the postmodern phenomenon and bewildering discrepancies between the ways many of these authors understand the term *postmodern* and its cognates."[6] Put very simply, postmodern thought can be seen in architecture, read in literature, pondered in philosophy, and heard in theology. It can be seen as a reaction against modernity and all that the Enlightenment birthed. Or, in a more positive light, it can be accepted as the next *Zeitgeist*, relinquishing the rigid shackles of its rational predecessor. For the purposes of this book, I

---

[5] Daniel L. Migliore, *Faith Seeking Understanding: An Introduction to Christian Theology* (Grand Rapids: Eerdmans, 1991) 238.
[6] Paul Lakeland, *Postmodernity: Christian Identity in a Fragmented Age* (Minneapolis: Fortress Press, 1997).

employ some postmodern thought to the interpretation of U2's lyrics. This work is not close-ended. Rather, it is available to be a catalyst for further discussion about the interplay between U2's songs and theology.

My hope is that this book will be of interest to U2 fans, offering them perhaps another perspective on U2's lyrics. I would also hope that those who are Christian, or religious, would recognize that the marriage of theology, faith, and popular culture is not only possible, but relevant and fruitful as well.

1
Poets for Turbulent Times

*"That the scriptures are brim full of hustlers, murderers, cowards, adulterers
and merceneries used to shock me; now it is a source of great comfort."*
—Bono[1]

Back in the late seventies, while only teenagers, Bono (Paul Hewson), Adam
Clayton, Larry Mullen Jr., and The Edge (Dave Evans) began their launch into
the music industry in Dublin, Ireland. Starting off with garage band names
such as "Feedback" and "The Hype," the boys settled on "U2," the name of an
American spy plane that had crashed into Soviet territory. At some early stages
in the band's development, its name almost foreshadowed its own ruin.

After their second album *October*, Bono, Larry, and Edge were at a
crossroads in their lives. They became involved in a charismatic Christian
group called Shalom. Shalom started innocently enough as a loose
gathering of charismatic Christians who read the scriptures and prayed.
After time, however, Shalom began to show signs of becoming what
appeared to be a shepherding group, where a core leadership had a great
amount of influence over the everyday lives of the community.[2] The leaders

---

[1] Bono, Introduction to *Selections from the Book of Psalms* (New York: Grove Press, 1999) xi.
[2] H. D. Hunter, "Shepherding Movement," *Dictionary of the Pentecostal and Charismatic
Movements* (Grand Rapids: Zondervan, 1988) 783–85.

of the movement gave the three band members an ultimatum: Renounce U2 and the "worldly" lifestyle, or be renounced by Shalom. "Shalom was prepared to accept the positive side of . . . Bono, Larry, and Edge's commitment, but not the music and culture that went with it."[3] Evidently, although not without much inner wrestling, the three opted for U2. What is more, the three decided for friendship as well. Bass player Adam Clayton, along with manager Paul McGuiness, wanted nothing to do with Shalom or religion. Though many have viewed Clayton as peripheral to the band, I would argue that he was the key to U2's success. Had Adam been involved with Shalom, U2 would have most likely become a second rate band trapped in the Christian music ghetto. Despite some minor frictions among the members, they decided to continue together.

The band did not become an overnight success. Rather, with hard work and the help of Paul McGuiness, U2 made consistent progress in the last twenty years, climbing the music charts and pushing the boundaries of rock and roll. Childhood dreams and expectations gave this Irish rock band deep longings to leave its unique mark on the world. Little did they realize that two decades later their careers would be compared with those of the Beatles and the Rolling Stones. With Bono's distinct vocals, Edge's innovative guitar techniques (which helped rescue rock from a techno era), and the band's profound lyrics, U2 has made and continues to make an impact in the world. In fact, nominated for eight Grammies in 2002, on February 27, U2 won four of those awards including Record of the Year ("Walk On") and Best Rock Album (*All That You Can't Leave Behind*) not to mention additional Grammies in 2005 for their latest success, "Vertigo." Here is a rock and roll group recognized the world over whose every album grapples with absorbing theological issues.

This book will wrestle with the biblical truths that permeate the songs of U2. Employing categories borrowed from Old Testament scholar Walter Brueggemann as an interpretive lens, it will examine the themes of hope amidst despair, social justice and eschatological anticipation, exile in a scorched land, and, lastly, grace and resurrection. In his book *Finally Comes the Poet*, Brueggemann poses the questions, "Is there another way to speak? Is there another voice to be voiced? Is there an alternative universe of discourse

---

[3] Eamon Dunphy, *Unforgettable Fire: Past, Present, and Future—The Definitive Biography of U2* (New York: Warner, 1988) 167.

to be practiced that will struggle with the truth in ways unreduced?"[4] The unreduced truth Brueggemann writes of is the biblical text, more specifically, the gospel. The medium of rock and roll music allows the artist to express raw emotion and high intellect simultaneously. It meshes these two into a potent poetry. This poetry, especially in a postmodern culture, opens a new door in Brueggemann's room of alternative discourse. I contend that through its music, U2 opens up that alternative universe of discourse, allowing its listeners to struggle with the truth in fresh and exciting ways.

Bono's Epistle

A little over a year into their career, U2 was on tour in England. During this time Bono wrote a compelling letter to his father (Bob Hewson). A portion of it reads:

> You should be aware that at the moment three of the group are committed Christians. That means offering each day up to God, meeting in the morning for prayers, readings, and letting God work in our lives. This gives us the strength and a joy that does not depend on drink or drugs. This strength will, I believe, be the quality that will take us to the top of the music business where never before have so many lost and sorrowful people gathered in one place pretending they're having a good time. *It is our ambition to make more than good music.*[5]

In retrospect, this segment of Bono's letter could arguably be interpreted as the band's mandate and faith. In line with the book of James in the New Testament, Richard Bauckham and Trevor Hart understand faith to be an outward expression more than an internal conviction. James writes:

> What good is it, my brothers and sisters, if you say you have faith but do not have works? Can faith save you? If a brother or sister is naked and lacks daily food, and one of you says to them, "Go in peace; keep

---

[4] Walter Brueggemann, *Finally Comes the Poet: Daring Speech for Proclamation* (Minneapolis: Fortress Press, 1989) 2.

[5] Bill Flanagan, *U2 at the End of the World* (New York, New York: Delacorte, 1995) 524 (italics mine).

warm and eat your fill," and yet you do not supply their bodily needs, what is the good of that? So faith by itself, if it has no works, is dead. (James 2:14-17)

Faith is expressed "by immersing ourselves actively in the very midst of the world's darkest and most depraved corners as salt and light with potentially transforming impact."[6] Alongside their altruistic causes (e.g., Artists Against Apartheid, Amnesty International, Greenpeace, Jubilee 2000, Drop the Debt Campaign, The Burma Project, DATA, The ONE Campaign, et al.), U2, through their songs, enter those very places (e.g., the Grammy Awards and the like) as salt and light.[7]

Two decades after its genesis, the band's lofty ambition is continuing to be realized. The four Irishmen have generated more than good music. They have sown poetic seeds of hope with transformative power. This is proven through lead singer and U2 frontman Bono, who has earned the ear and respect of such notable figures as Pope John Paul II, Bill Clinton, Jean Chretien, George Soros, Jesse Helms, Colin Powell, George W. Bush, Paul Martin, Bill Gates, as well the United Nations.[8] The spiritual strength Bono referred to in his letter not only brought the band to the top of the music business, but it has also propelled them to the forefront of a global political arena. Indeed, U2 is earning as great a respected voice in the political sphere as it enjoys in the music and entertainment industry.

U2 and a Postmodern Political World

Beyond the painful veneer of the music industry, U2's music wanders the dark corners of a postmodern world, a "labyrinth of endless play" whose

---

[6] Richard Bauckham and Trevor Hart, *Hope Against Hope: Christian Eschatology at the Turn of the Millennium* (Grand Rapids: Eerdmans, 1999) 82.

[7] *Propaganda: U2 World Service Magazine*, summer 2000, issue 1, vol.2. "November 13, 1999: Bono joins Marilyn Manson for an impromptu jam with Iggy Pop after the MTV Music Awards in Dublin," 3. Just one of many examples of U2 visiting one of the world's dark and depraved corners. From grief-stricken Africa to the glamorous award shows, both can be described as poor: Financial poverty on the one hand vs. poverty of the soul on the other.

[8] Josh Tyrangiel, "Bono's Mission," *Time*, 4 March 2002, 60–67.

tenants have "abandoned belief in the existence of a way out . . . or a golden thread to lead [them out]."[9] It is a place that is "characterized by a loss of belief in an objective world and an incredulity towards meta-narratives of legitimation . . . There is no foundation to secure a universal and objective *reality*."[10] Songs saturated with the gospel story offer the postmodern resident a cup of refreshing water: centeredness in exchange for displacement, hope in place of despair.

It is quite ironic that U2, a multi-million dollar philanthropic rock band, is giving advice to global leaders on how to handle their finances, encouraging debt forgiveness of two thirds of the world's countries. A rock and roll group is generally associated with entertainment, not human rights. What right does a jester have to counsel the royal court about mammon and God? Yet this is precisely what U2 does, and with bravado. United States Treasury Secretary Paul O'Neill commented on his first meeting with Bono, "'I refused to meet him at first . . . I thought he was just some pop star who wanted to use me.' After their scheduled half-hour session went ninety minutes, O'Neill changed his mind."[11] Bono himself admits "how absurd it is to have a rock star talk about the World Health Organization or debt relief or HIV/AIDS in Africa." Yet as *Time's* Josh Tyrangiel points out, "no one else with [Bono's] kind of access to media and money has taken on the job."[12] I would add that Bono is directed by his spiritual compulsion that propels him towards issues of social justice.

Walter Brueggemann writes that "speech about hope must be primally theological . . . It will finally be about God and us, about his faithfulness that vetoes our faithlessness. Those who would be prophetic will need to embrace that absurd practice and that subversive activity."[13] In line with Brueggemann's thought on hope and subversive activity, Bono says:

> I'm trying to be embarrassable. I think that may be our job. I want to say these things that people are thinking and not saying. Things have got very constricted. I think it's the job of the singer: to fess up to the

---

[9] Bauckham and Hart, *Hope Against Hope*, 61.
[10] Walter Truett Anderson, ed. *The Truth About the Truth: De-confusing and Re-constructing the Postmodern World* (New York: Tarcher/Putnam, 1995) 19.
[11] Tyrangiel, "Bono's Mission," 62.
[12] Ibid.
[13] Brueggemann, *The Prophetic Imagination*, 65.

stuff. I want to make a record that does that, that's nonsense and makes sense . . . the Death and Resurrection show.[14]

Brueggemann would agree with Bono's job description. He writes that "if the [biblical] text is to claim authority it will require neither the close reasoning of a canon lawyer, nor the precision of a technician, but it will require an artist to render the text in quite fresh ways, so that the text breaks life open."[15] That, according to Bono, is what the singer does. As an artist the singer enters a constricted reality where the biblical text is suppressed. This is a self-proclaimed reality whose *condition is without a sense of the future.*[16] Upon entering that world, the singer is called to honest proclamation, or in Bono's words, "Fessing up to the stuff."

That honesty takes on different forms. For example, for the purposes of avoiding being labeled "rocker against bad things," Bono's passion for the African continent is displayed somberly in political back rooms. Standing in front of sold-out stadiums, however, the singer openly prays Eugene Peterson's rendering of Psalm 116, "What can I give back to [God] for the blessings he's poured out on me? What can I give back to [God] for the blessings he's poured out on me? I'll lift high the cup of salvation—a toast to [our Father]!"[17] Both the politicking and prayers fulfill Bono's calling to honest proclamation.

U2's music unabashedly confronts a constructed, constricted reality by rendering the biblical text in refreshing ways. Richard Middleton and Brian Walsh rightly observe that Western reality is "one of holes in the ozone layer, rampant environmental destruction, debilitating poverty, and worldwide inequity, oppression and terror. It is a reality of abuse, loneliness, fear and perpetual threat."[18] The authors continue that, "when confronted with the reality we have constructed, we are brought face to face with our arrogance—with our own brokenness, ambiguity and evil."[19]

---

[14] Chris Heath, "U2: Band of the Year," *Rolling Stone*, 18 January 2001, 36.

[15] Brueggemann, *Finally Comes the Poet*, 9.

[16] Bauckham and Hart, *Hope Against Hope*, 61. The authors here describe the condition of postmodernity (italics mine).

[17] Eugene H. Peterson, *The Message: Psalms* (Ps. 116), see also "Where the Streets Have No Name" on *U2: Elevation 2001/U2 Live from Boston*, Universal, 2001. DVD.

[18] J. Richard Middleton and Brian J. Walsh, *Truth is Stranger than it Used to Be* (Illinois: IVP, 1995) 37.

[19] Ibid.

I would argue that U2's music confronts its listeners with the reality they (the listeners) have constructed, and brings them face to face with the world's own arrogance, brokenness, ambiguity, and evil. U2 also lyrically construct an alternative reality, which they invite their listeners to inhabit. This is the heart of all rich communication, not least the communication known as proclaiming the gospel and shaping a prophetic imagination.

Brueggemann says that biblical poetry "assaults [the] imagination and pushes out the presumed world in which most of us are trapped."[20] At its best, that is what U2's music does. In an interview with *Rolling Stone* Bono admits:

> Talking about big ideas like God and sex and death and family . . . I want to talk about them. I'm not going to *not* talk about them . . . I don't know anyone who's not interested in the idea of religion, either whether they're opposed to it or for it. Yet no one talks about it. It's taboo. People will talk about penis rings easier at a dinner table these days than the idea of grace.[21]

Bono concurs with Brueggemann that God-language has the power to assault the imagination. It is because of the dense theological language of hope in U2's album *All That You Can't Leave Behind* that Americans gravitated to its songs after September 11, 2001. Released in November of 2000, *ATYCLB* eerily had, among other symbols, a 747 jet soaring through the air (seen especially in the Elevation Tour Book and on T-shirts). Videos of the album's three most popular tracks ("Beautiful Day," "Elevation," and "Walk On") each begin with a 747 roaring in the background. Certainly the album is not prescient, only intuitive. The plane represents unlimited imagination (i.e., "the sky's the limit"). It is not conceivable that U2 would ever have used a 747 post September 11, 2001. Since the image was employed prior to the terrorist attacks, the right is theirs to reclaim the plane as a symbol of hope, instead of terror.

One week after the September 11 tragedy, artists gathered together for a global telethon to raise funds for the families of the victims. U2

---

[20] Brueggemann, *Finally Comes the Poet*, 3.
[21] Heath, "U2: Band of the Year," 41.

chose to perform "Walk On." In a prophetic manner, Bono sang, "Leave it behind."

The song did not end like its album version. Defiantly, in a chorus of hallelujahs, Bono shouted to the departed souls, "I'll see you when I get home!" Only U2 would have been able to get away with singing this song so defiantly. Of all the sets that evening, "Walk On" was the only song that not only addressed suffering and loss, but also dealt with letting go, leaving behind, and moving forward in hope.

U2 and the Psalmist/Prophet

If the prophet Jeremiah were present today, what form would he take: A televangelist or a rock star? Perhaps in seeking an audience with current political leadership, he would replace his wooden yoke with a gaudy costume and bug-eyed sunglasses. If the psalmists walked today's concrete hills, would their songs be confined to the lips of the elite, or would everyday people be humming those tunes as prayers to God? I am not suggesting that Bono or U2 are actual modern day prophets declaring, "Thus saith the Lord!" What I do propose is that U2 speaks in the spirit of an Old Testament prophet when confronting the regimes of this age or when offering hope to the afflicted through its music. Eugene Peterson, one of Bono's favorite authors, puts it this way, "Prophets confront us with the sovereign presence of God in our lives . . . Amos crafted poems, Jeremiah wept sermons, Isaiah alternately rebuked and comforted, Ezekiel did street theater. U2 writes songs and goes on tour, singing them."[22] What U2 and the prophets share is an imagination and a willingness to use their gifts to clothe themselves and their message in whatever forms will help it be heard most clearly and effectively.

According to Brueggemann, "God needs prophets [/poets] in order to make himself known, and all prophets are necessarily artistic. What a prophet has to say can never be said in prose."[23] U2's political clout does not stem from its social activism. On the contrary, U2's sense of social

---

[22] Beth Maynard and Raewynne J. Whiteley, eds., *Get Up Off Your Knees: Preaching the U2 Catalog,* with a foreword by Eugene Peterson (Cambridge: Cowley, 2003), xii.
[23] Brueggemann, *Finally Comes the Poet,* 4.

justice is fed by the powerful truths of their music. Granted, Bono does not sing or write Hebrew poetry, but he comes close to its raw passion. In his introduction to a pocket version of the Psalms, Bono writes: "Words and music did for me what solid, even rigorous, religious argument could never do, they introduced me to God, not belief in God, more an experiential sense of GOD. Over art, literature, reason, the way to my spirit was a combination of words and music."[24]

The Psalms have been a definite influence on U2's music. One of the band's first singles was titled "A Celebration," and it is reminiscent of such praise psalms as Psalms 135, 148, 149, and 150. U2's second album, *October*, contains songs such as "Gloria" and "Scarlet," whose only lyric is the refrain "Rejoice." The song sung by audiences worldwide at the close of many U2 concerts is "40." Referring to the *War* album, Bono reminisces:

> We wanted to put something explicitly spiritual on the record to balance the politics and the romance of it . . . "40" became the closing song at U2 shows and on hundreds of occasions, literally thousands of people . . . have shouted back the refrain, pinched from Psalm 6: "How long (to sing this song)." I had thought of it as a nagging question—pulling at the hem of an invisible deity whose presence we glimpse only when we act in love. How long . . . hunger? How long . . . hatred? How long until creation grows up and the chaos of its precocious, hell-bent adolescence has been discarded? I thought it odd that the vocalising of such questions could bring such comfort.[25]

With resonances from Paul's letter to the believers in Rome, Bono's comments on "40" lead nicely into U2's understanding of social justice and eschatology, as will be discussed in chapter three of this book.[26]

"40," based on Psalm 40, was not the last song influenced by the Psalms. "Wake up Dead Man" is a less hopeful song that tightly parallels Psalm 44. Treating God somewhat roughly, as the psalmist did, Bono

---

[24] Bono, Introduction to *Selections from the Book of Psalms*, ix.

[25] Ibid., xi–xii.

[26] Paul writes: "Creation itself will be set free from its bondage to decay and will obtain the freedom of the glory of the children of God. We know that the whole creation has been groaning in labor pains until now" (Rom 8:21-22).

says, "People want to believe but they're angry. If God is not dead, there's some questions we want to ask him."[27] Those questions are similar to the ones the psalmist refused to back away from.

> Rouse yourself! Why do you sleep, O Lord?
> Awake, do not cast us off forever!
> Why do you hide your face?
> Why do you forget our affliction and oppression? (Psalm 44:23-24)

The prophet's call to honest proclamation spills over into his relationship with Yahweh.[28] This idea of being blunt with God will be further discussed in chapter four, *The Babylonian State of Zooropa.*

Trying to Throw Your Arms around U2

To improve an understanding of the Psalms, Brueggemann turns to Paul Ricoeur and borrows the idea of the dynamic of life as a movement.[29] Ricoeur suggests that "two movements in human life are important: (*a*) deep reluctance to let loose of a world that has passed away, and (*b*) capacity to embrace a new world being given."[30] Brueggemann extends this thought and proposes the sequence of *orientation-disorientation-reorientation* to help understand how the Psalms might have functioned in the life of Israel.[31]

Psalms of orientation would include wisdom psalms where everything in creation is in order. God is sovereign, the righteous are blessed, and the wicked are dealt with according to their crimes (e.g., Pss. 104, 127, 128, 131, 133, 145). The sequence, however, cannot remain here. The place of orientation does not quite suffice. As Bauckham and Hart acknowledge,

---

[27] Niall Stokes, *Into the Heart: The Stories Behind Every U2 Song* (Dubai: Carlton, 2001) 139.

[28] Consider Jeremiah's abrasive speech towards Yahweh: "O LORD, you have enticed me, and I was enticed; you have overpowered me, and you prevailed. I have become a laughingstock all day long; everyone mocks me" (Jer 20:7).

[29] Brueggemann, *The Psalms and the Life of Faith* (Minneapolis: Fortress Press, 1995) 8.

[30] Paul Ricoeur, *Biblical Hermeneutics*, (1975) 114–24.

[31] Ibid., 9.

"Humans . . . are essentially insatiable, driven forwards by a desire for contact with a reality the fullness of which constantly eludes us."[32] That yearning for the divine cannot be satisfied in the territory of orientation. In order for a person to get beyond orientation towards something greater, disorientation occurs, for the most part against the person's will.

The fact that a yearning exists indicates that the orientation is, to some degree, shallow. At deeper levels there is a spiritual malaise or restlessness. The temptation is to try to escape by moving from the depths to the shallows, which can never work because we bring the malaise with us. The psalmists and the prophets and, especially, Jesus know that the only way out is through. They plunge into the depths of disorientation and suffering, clinging always to the firm hope that joy is deeper than suffering.

Psalms of disorientation include psalms of lament. "[These] psalms remember better times (Ps 42:4) back in the old period of orientation. There is a wish to return to that situation. Others are heavy in anger and resentment against the one who has caused disorientation . . . This mood leaves the impression that the speaker believes that the loss of orientation is reversible and the old orientation is retrievable."[33] An excellent example of disorientation is Psalm 88. Brueggemann highlights that "Psalm 88 is unrelieved in its embrace of disorientation: there is no movement away from displacement."[34] Psalm 44 (mentioned above) is another prime example of disorientation. The song ends not with rescue, but with despair and confusion. "God, why can't it be like the days of old? Why do you no longer shame our enemies? Why can't we boast in your name all day long? Wake up Dead Man!"

Enter the "new songs," or psalms of reorientation! This part of the sequence is not a return to "the good old days." On the contrary, reorientation is new, hopeful, and imaginative. What was once impossible is now possible: "Grace makes beauty out of ugly things."[35] Brueggemann names psalms of thanksgiving and praise as new or reoriented (e.g., Pss

---

[32] Bauckham and Hart, *Hope Against Hope*, 52.
[33] Brueggemann, *The Psalms and the Life of Faith*, 11.
[34] Ibid., 13.
[35] "Grace," from the album *All That You Can't Leave Behind*. © 2000 Universal International Music BV.

13, 30, 40, 138).[36] Hannah's song (1 Sam 2:1-10) and the Magnificat (Luke 1:46-55) should also be included. Yahweh has delivered, victoriously succeeded, and surprised. For the person in disorientation, reorientation is not anticipated. It arrives suddenly and surprisingly, without predictability, and is to be received as a radical gift. The only fitting response is amazement.

Though the psalms reflect experience, they are necessarily somewhat stylized and idealized. It is not always easy to reconstruct the experience with any precision, nor to know how to apply a psalm to contemporary life. Just so, it can be somewhat daunting to try to set U2's musical history in this theological construction. Nevertheless, the use of Brueggemann's typology can prove useful in appreciating the theological depth of U2's music. When employed as an interpretive lens, the structure of orientation, disorientation, and reorientation has a certain heuristic power. Not only are the dynamics of Brueggemann's typology found within the sequence of U2's albums, but they are also observed within specific songs (e.g., "Where the Streets Have No Name," and "I Still Haven't Found What I'm Looking For," which will be looked at in chapter three).

A brief overview of the sequence of U2's albums will help illustrate the point. After the release of U2's most popular album, *The Joshua Tree*, the members of U2 compared *The Joshua Tree* with its predecessor, *The Unforgettable Fire* (released 1984). Edge recognizes *The Joshua Tree* as an extension of *The Unforgettable Fire*, which he describes as a beautifully impressionistic record that was out of focus. *The Joshua Tree* is in focus. He contrasts songs with similar themes on both albums pointing out the ambiguity of one and the clarity of the other (e.g., "A Sort of Homecoming" with "In God's Country," and "Bad" with "Where the Streets Have No Name").[37] Musically as well as lyrically, *The Joshua Tree* fits into the category of orientation. Despite several subversive songs, the band and its audience know where everybody stands. *The Joshua Tree* was soon followed by a live album (*Rattle and Hum*), movie (*Rattle and Hum*), and book (*The Unforgettable Fire* by Eamon Dunphy). At the level of success, fame, and finances, all was well. Yet the truth of "I Still Haven't Found What I'm

---

[36] Brueggemann, *The Message of the Psalms: A Theological Commentary* (Minneapolis: Augsburg, 1984) 122–67.
[37] Mark Taylor, *U2* (Italy: Carlton, 1996) with interview CD.

Looking For" remained. Besides, the media blitz that accompanied the band's success, along with U2's outspokenness on social issues, led many to think they were too egoistic and self-righteous. Labeled megalomaniacs, U2 retreated after their Love Town Tour (associated with *Rattle and Hum*).

This snub by the critics instigated a three-album response by U2. From 1991 to 1997 the band released *Achtung Baby* (1991), *Zooropa* (1993), and *Pop* (1997). This trilogy is a harrowing journey into the stereotype of decadent rock and roll. Gaudy costumes and ridiculous antics (on- and offstage) accompanied a harsher, less forgiving U2 sound. The albums are replete with irony and satire. In relation to *The Joshua Tree*, the trilogy is disorienting. Yet the songs are not without a message. Regarding the title and album *Achtung Baby*, Bono confesses:

> It's a con. It's just a way of putting people off from the fact that it's a heavy 'mother.' It's probably our most serious record and yet it's the least serious title. And it just fooled everyone. They thought we all lightened up, which is totally untrue. We're miserable bastards.[38]

The trilogy outlines the hopelessness of a postmodern, consumer-driven world. The final track on *Pop* is titled "Wake Up Dead Man" and, as mentioned earlier, is a parallel to Psalm 44, a psalm of disorientation. The trilogy concludes in despair and confusion.

U2 followed *Pop* with two other albums, *All That You Can't Leave Behind* (*ATYCLB*) and their latest album *How to Dismantle an Atomic Bomb* (*HTDAAB*). *ATYCLB* is an album brimming with joy, hope, and surprise. Songs such as "Beautiful Day," "Walk On," and "Grace" demand the listener's imagination to venture beyond a bleak world into a new existence full of life and glorious anticipation. *HTDAAB* continues in the vein of reorientation. In this album we hear prayers thinly disguised as rock songs. The prayers are heard in songs like "Vertigo," "Love and Peace or Else," "All Because of You," and "Yahweh." *ATYCLB* along with *HTDAAB* are U2's albums of reorientation. It is with this understanding of U2's discography that I intend to exegete their songs.

---

[38] Bono, "Achtung Baby: the Videos, the Cameos and a Whole Lot of Interference from Zoo TV", videocassette.© 1991 Island/Polygram.

Before doing so, however, I think it would be wise to revisit Bono's love for the Psalms. In particular, it is important to note and remember that Bono has always had a passion for the lament psalms, and, therefore, U2's music and lyrics are full of longing passion. Even in *The Joshua Tree*, which I describe as an album of orientation, there is never a sure sense of settled, arrived orientation. Instead, orientation is envisioned and hoped for—and even celebrated—in the midst of the moments of disorientation. U2 always seems to be singing "How long?" *The Joshua Tree* holds a tension between orientation and disorientation. Since U2's audience did not fully comprehend or accept this disorientation, the band launched into a deeper disorientation. Allow me to add some final comments on interpreting U2's lyrics.

U2's License for Lyrical Interpretation

"Bongolese, as Daniel Lanois calls it, is coming through the loudspeakers in a recording studio on the riverside in Dublin where a new U2 album is being born." Both Daniel Lanois (producer) and Edge have notebooks in hand, "but as they try to decipher the taped language of the singer, each is transcribing a different lyric. Even if they can't agree on an interpretation between them, the duo transcribe what they believe are the words corresponding to the sound of Bono's voice and try to develop the phrasing."[39] Without going off on a tangent on all the postmodern language that could be employed to describe how these two colleagues construct their own realities, I take some comfort from the fact that two professional musicians and songwriters who have known Bono for many years still have difficulty decoding his lyrics.

Just as Lanois' hearings in U2's studio differ from Edge's, my understanding of certain songs may not correspond with someone else's. Yet particular songs have irrefutable ties to the Scriptures (e.g., as noted above, "40" with Psalm 40, and "Wake Up Dead Man" with Psalm 44). Without abusing the lyrics of U2's songs, chapters 2–6 expound upon their meaning while still remaining within the boundaries of dialogue

---

[39] Martin Wroe, *Propaganda: U2 World Service Magazine*, summer 2000, issue 1, vol.2, 12.

that the band has initiated with its listeners (perhaps stretching those boundaries just a bit).

What I am concerned with is the meaning behind these lyrics. Can a song have more than one meaning? I would argue that it could. The members of U2 agree. In an interview with Alan Light, one month after September 11, 2001, U2 rethinks the meaning behind certain songs.

> **Edge:** Every lyric takes on a whole new meaning, especially a song like "I Still Haven't Found What I'm Looking For," which we hadn't played for a good few years. And a song like "Peace on Earth"—when we finished our record, I was surprised at how certain themes were so strong, a certain sense of mortality, of trying to cope with loss.

> **Mullen:** "Beautiful Day" takes on a whole different meaning, [because] that was the thing on September 11—it *was* a beautiful morning. It could have been a video, the beautiful day being destroyed.

> **Bono:** . . . The songs can completely change their meanings. It's wild how a song can change. I really learned that from listening to Sinatra, because he didn't write lyrics, but he turned them on their head. Like one of the last versions he ever sang of "My Way"—it's a duet with Pavarotti, and it's no longer a boast, it's an apology. Same lyric.[40]

Larry Mullen Jr. was a little annoyed when Bono collaborated with longtime friend and editor, Niall Stokes. Stokes compiled a book that "explained" the lyrics of every U2 song. Stokes' book (*Into the Heart*) is used as an aid in my interpretation, and I am grateful for his contribution to the growing library of all things U2. However, focusing primarily on brief anecdotal histories of the songs, Stokes generally refuses to allow any theological interpretation to break into his reflections. Speaking with *Time*, Larry shares his frustration about the book and reveals that one of the most valuable things about Bono's lyrics is their adaptability "to any particular situation."[41]

---

[40] Alan Light, "Band of the Year: Rock's Unbreakable Heart," *Spin*, January 2002, 58.
[41] Tyrangiel, "Bono's Mission," 66.

This book will demonstrate that the music of U2 intertwines Scripture, theology, and rock music in a unique thread. The band offers this thread to its postmodern culture as a gift, a hope, a way out of the maze. As mentioned at the beginning of this chapter, viewed through the interpretive lens provided by Brueggemann, we will examine the undeniable biblical themes of hope amidst despair, social justice and eschatological anticipation, exile in a scorched land, grace and resurrection, and, lastly, prayers for the journey home.

2
Songs of Hope for the Drowning

"Hope comes close to being the very heart and centre of a human being."
—William F. Lynch[1]

*"The hope that's in the music comes from the hope that's in the band. I
believe it's time to fight back in your spirit—right down deep inside.
There is a great faith in this group."*
—Bono[2]

Lost at sea. The image conjures up emotions of fear, vulnerability, and
hopelessness. But what if, while slowly slipping under in the middle of a
dark cold ocean, the drowning one is thrown a life preserver of surprise?
This chapter will examine two stimulating songs written by U2 at different
periods in their career. Each of the songs plays with the metaphors of
drowning and rescue. In essence, the message of these songs, though written

---

[1] William F. Lynch, *Images of Hope: Imagination as Healer of the Hopeless* (Dublin: Helicon, 1965) 21.
[2] James Henke, "Blessed are the Peacemakers," *Rolling Stone*, 9 June 1983, *U2: The Rolling Stone Files* (New York: Hyperion, 1994) 16.

17

at various times, is the same. From 1983 with "Drowning Man" (*War*), to 1991 with "Until the End of the World" (*Achtung Baby*), U2 declares an incredulous message of hope in the midst of impossibility.

These two songs tell the story of two individuals overwhelmed by a tumultuous, inescapable storm. In the latter song the storm is the hopelessness that leads to suicide. However bleak the circumstance, God breaks in with suddenness and surprise. "Real hope is essentially rooted in the qualities and capacities of otherness . . . It is, in Lynch's words, 'an interior sense that there is help on the outside of us.'"[3] The afflicted subject of the song breathes in a new imagination that allows for this real hope— a hope that the listener can also catch.

Drowning Man

In 1983, U2 had released its third album, *War*. Containing such recognized songs as "Sunday Bloody Sunday" (a commentary on the troubles in Northern Ireland) and "New Year's Day" (dealing with Poland's governmental upheaval), *War* was U2's first political album. This was a marked contrast from their first two albums, *Boy*, which dealt with the transitions of adolescence to adulthood, and *October*, which was explicitly, even pointedly Christian.

War's fifth track, "Drowning Man," is not a song one typically thinks of during this stage of U2's journey. Though seldom included in the popular "U2 canon," "Drowning Man" is a hidden pearl on the album. Of it, the Edge says: "Whereas I know some of the songs on the *War* album could be re-recorded and improved on, with 'Drowning Man' it's perfection for that song. It's one of the most successful pieces of recording we've ever done."[4] Resonating with hope, the song is sung from God's perspective. He extends his hand to a person overwhelmed by the raging waves of a stormy ocean.

Without giving much detail, Stokes comments that "Drowning Man" is "a song written from the perspective of a loving God. It may, in its way, be entirely presumptuous—but, far more importantly, its cup is overflowing with tenderness. And it is addressed to Adam Clayton."[5] At

---

[3] Bauckham and Hart, *Hope Against Hope*, 62.
[4] Stokes, *Into the Heart*, 43.
[5] Ibid.

an early point in their careers, Adam was fearful of losing his status as U2's bassist because he wasn't a Christian. His bout with alcohol did not help either. The media began to label Adam as "a vicious drunk."[6] Yet the fraternal bond of this band remained secure, and "Drowning Man," as intense as it is, is a token of friendship and love towards Adam.

Bono hesitantly refers to "Drowning Man" as a psalm.[7] This "psalm," however, does not speak in the person of any ordinary psalmist. It is God or Yahweh himself addressing a person to whom he has bestowed his love and kindness. A conversation develops when "Drowning Man" is set beside Psalm 13. The psalm begins with a series of desperate cries in the form of rhetorical questions, followed by petitions for help:

> How much longer, LORD,
>> will you forget about me?
> Will it be forever?
>> How long will you hide?
> How long must I be confused
>> and miserable all day?
> How long will my enemies
>> keep beating me down?
> Please listen, LORD God,
>> and answer my prayers.
> Make my eyes sparkle again,
> or else I will fall
>> into the sleep of death. (Psalm 13:1-3, CEV)

Though desperate, this psalmist has not completely abandoned all hope. He can still imagine that God will rescue him; and it is precisely such imagination and openness to the future that characterize hope. "With its eyes wide open to the threat which the future holds, [hope] nonetheless sees ways of averting this threat."[8] The psalmist realizes his hope can be founded in no other power save God. Despair and distress are circling him. Only God has the ability to revitalize his life and restore that light to

---

[6] Henke, "Blessed are the Peacemakers," 15.

[7] Stokes, *Into the Heart*, 43.

[8] Bauckham and Hart, *Hope Against Hope*, 53.

the eye. Imagine Yahweh's response to the psalmist in the words of U2: *Take my hand, you know I'll be there.*[9]

Although Bono had Adam in mind when writing "Drowning Man," the song takes on a wider meaning because of its position within the *War* album. "Like a Song," the fourth track on *War*, reveals the band's frustration with society's *laissez-faire* attitude. The song is addressed to and identifies U2's generation: *A generation without name, ripped and torn.*[10] No longer is it Adam who is "encompassed by the cords of death"[11]; it is a generation ripped and torn, imprisoned, and rendered nothing in a postmodern culture.

Borrowed from Isaiah 40, the closing lines of "Drowning Man" provide the listener with important interpretive clues.[12] The second part of the book of Isaiah addresses Judah following a time of political chaos, war, and exile. The kingdom of Babylon had conquered Judah. The hallmark of Babylon's strategy in building its empire was the assimilation of defeated kingdoms. The Babylonian army would strip a city of its elite and march them in chains back to Babylon. Any identity or concept of home was stripped away. The exiles, being uprooted, were to become docile members of a "greater" kingdom, being allowed to contribute through agriculture and trade.[13] The despair of the exiles is heard through Isaiah's voice earlier in the chapter when he writes,

> All people are grass,
> their constancy is like the flower of the field.
> The grass withers, the flower fades,
> when the breath of the LORD blows upon it;
> surely the people are grass. (Isaiah 40:6b-7)

Explaining the idea of being uprooted, Middleton and Walsh write:

> The postmodern self thus finds itself ultimately homeless. The notion of
> a settled home or a stable world is, after all, an illusory modern (and

---

[9] "Drowning Man," from the album *War*. © 1983 Island Records Ltd.

[10] "Like a Song," from the album *War*. © 1983 Island Records Ltd.

[11] See Psalms 18: 4-6; 116:3-4, and Matthew 14:22-33.

[12] "But those who wait for the LORD shall renew their strength, they shall mount up with wings like eagles, they shall run and not be weary, they shall walk and not faint." Isaiah 40:31.

[13] Brueggemann's interpretation of "exile" will be more closely examined in chapter 4, "The Babylonian State of Zooropa."

premodern) construction that can no longer be believed. So, the emerging postmodern vision disallows any such settledness for human life.[14]

That is the storm of winds and tides that threatens to drag away the postmodern generation. A vessel without an anchor is easily swept away. Homelessness is a serious problem of the postmodern condition. U2 aptly intuits this condition in its song "Stateless": *I've got no home in this world.*[15]

Postmodernism strips an individual of a future, of identity, of home, leaving *nothing to lose and nothing to gain, nothing at all.* What's the difference in a random world devoid of colour and purpose? What passion can there be if there is no race to run? What joy is left without sunshine? What hope without a tomorrow? Do we finally, as Middleton and Walsh suggest, "find ourselves enmeshed in a confusion of tongues, a bewildering cacophony of local agendas and perspectives?"[16] Are we trapped, forgotten in a world marred by "tribal warfare, cultural disintegration and homelessness, where the self is under siege?"[17] No. There is one outside of us with the power to break through the cultural tempest.

Yahweh sings a different song. He promises to be present in the storm, offering his hand, wondering if his child can accept this: *"Take my hand. You know I'll be there. If you can, I'll cross the sky for your love. Give you what I hold dear."* "Take my hand!" cries God.

> Can a woman forget her nursing child,
> or show no compassion for the child of her womb?
> Even these may forget,
> yet I will not forget you.
> See, I have inscribed you
> on the palms of my hands. (Isaiah 49:15-16a)

When reaching for Yahweh's hand, the drowning one sees her name forever cauterized on the palm his hand. She is not alone. She has not been

---

[14] Middleton and Walsh, *Truth is Stranger than it Used to Be*, 58.
[15] "Stateless," from the soundtrack *The Million Dollar Hotel.* © 2000 Universal Island Records Ltd.
[16] Middleton and Walsh, *Truth is Stranger than it Used to Be*, 172.
[17] Ibid.

forgotten. In the middle of the sea, she is not homeless, without identity. Her name has been inscribed on God himself.

What is it that God holds dear and gives to the troubled soul? What life preserver does he extend? It is more than the promise of rejuvenated strength to keep on enduring. What Yahweh holds dear is himself. He gives himself, his community, the gift to be included into his story. He offers his Son. To the drowning man, lost at sea, Yahweh offers security and a divine point of reference, a communal story to call one's own. This love, this covenant love lasts forever. Were the drowning man to respond to God's initiative, the paradigm shift of Psalm 13 would be appropriate:

> I trust your love,
> and I feel like celebrating
>   because you rescued me.
> You have been good to me, LORD,
>   and I will sing about you. (Psalm 13:5-6, CEV)

"Drowning Man" is a poem of hope. The song empowers the listener . . . "to move into the future, to transcend the present with its perceived limits and difficulties, to imagine a way out of that which constrains and threatens to engulf or imprison. Hope is that which insists on expanding our perceived horizons of possibility, broadening the landscape of reality in such a way as to set present circumstance in a wider perspective, thereby robbing it of its absoluteness."[18]

This song not only undermines the power of the storm, it also strips it of its absoluteness. It not only expands our horizons of possibility, but actually provides a horizon, a navigational orientation, where none had existed! It is God's reminder that, when all is said and done, the storm belongs to him.[19] Yahweh, who stands outside of history's control, rescues humanity from the "shipwreck of history."[20]

---

[18] Bauckham and Hart, *Hope Against Hope*, 54.

[19] Psalm 29 subverts the storm god Baal, and attributes true power to YHWH, enthroning him as King forever.

[20] Bauckham and Hart, *Hope Against*, 68. See also John Dominic Crossan, *The Dark Interval: Toward a Theology of Story* (Niles, Illinois: Argus, 1975) 44. "There is no lighthouse keeper. There is no lighthouse. There is no dry land. There are only people living on rafts made from their own imaginations. And there is the sea."

New Year's Day at the End of the World

"Until the End of the World," the fourth track of U2's critically acclaimed *Achtung Baby*, is a post-resurrection conversation between Judas and Jesus. Judas retells the story of their last encounter: *In waves of regret, waves of joy . . . You, you said you'd wait until the end of world.*[21] The song can be interpreted on two levels. First, it can be taken at face value as a conversation between a despondent Judas and a silent Jesus. A second option is to apply the image of bride and groom to the relationship between God and his people, between Christ and his Church. Hosea, Ephesians, and Revelation—to only name three—provide ample warrant for such an understanding. Of course, to do so, one must link the story of Judas (i.e., his loneliness, fear, crime, guilt, and eventual hope) to the story of the Church. The Gospels themselves make that link. On the one hand, Judas betrayed Christ. On the other hand, as Mark and Matthew emphasize, all of Jesus' disciples "deserted him and fled."[22] Feebly shadowing Jesus from alleyway to courtyard, eventually Peter also abandoned his Lord. So has the Church, so have we all. Bono is making precisely this connection.

The listener's imagination is required to set the context of the song. Judas is down in the hold or the brig of a ship. The ship is called Sheol, that is, Hades or death. Someone pays Judas a visit for the first time since he arrived. His visitor is Jesus, the man he is guilty of betraying. Ray Anderson muses as to what these two figures would say to one another. Here is an excerpt of the imagined conversation:

> You knew even then, did You not,
> that I was plotting to betray You?
> Why didn't You stop me—or at least expose me as a traitor?
>
> *I knew, but sought your love for Me by sharing My love for you.*
> *I have prayed for you Judas,*
> *that your love might return and that you might be healed.*

---

[21] "Until the End of the World," from the album *Achtung Baby.* © 1991 Island Records Ltd.
[22] Mark 14:50, Matthew 26:56.

I once prayed too. But no answers came.
If I cannot love and cannot pray, what hope is there?[23]

Essentially, that is the question for Judas in the song. "What hope is there for me?" The song is deliberately ambiguous. Judas does not elicit a response from Jesus, and the listener is left wondering about Judas' fate.

Despite its vague conclusion, "Until the End of the World" does offer enough hearty fodder for conjecture. At the end of each verse, a transition occurs where Christ is *talking* about the end of the world, *acting* like it was the end of the world, and *waiting* until the end of the world. The three verbs offer a line of thought through the song that walk the listener through the Last Supper, the betrayal in the Garden of Gethsemane, and finally the Consummation.

During the Last Supper, the disciples could not wrap their minds around the subject matter of Jesus' sermon. The "talking" refers to Christ's death. His death was not the ending of Christ's world. Instead Christ's death and resurrection marked the end of the reign of sin and death over creation. Jesus' presence in the dialogue demands a resurrection. Bauckham and Hart put it this way: "The resurrection of Jesus is the paradigm case for Christian hope. As Moltmann suggests, the relationship between the crucified Jesus and the risen Lord must therefore furnish the gestalt for imagining the relationship between the tragic limits of this world and the surprising, comic dimensions of God's new creation."[24] Judas in Sheol, a place that one can only imagine as being disorientating, is about to be thrown a life preserver. The resurrection of the very Christ he betrayed, will offer Judas an unimagined, unexpected, unfathomable hope. Is a second chance possible?

The second verse is an admission of guilt mixed with partial blame. *I took the money, I spiked your drink . . . you led me on.* The "acting" occurs in the Garden of Gethsemane. This is not the first occurrence of humanity playing the harlot. Jeremiah voices Yahweh's indictment on Israel for playing the harlot.

---

[23] Ray S. Anderson, *The Gospel According to Judas: Is There a Limit to God's Forgiveness?* (Colorado Springs: NavPress, 1991) 44.

[24] Bauckham and Hart, *Hope Against Hope*, 69.

On every high hill
    and under every green tree
you sprawled and played the whore . . .
How can you say, "I am not
    defiled,
I have not gone after the
    Baals"?
Look at your way in the valley;
    know what you have done—
a restive young camel interlacing
    her tracks,
a wild ass at home in the
    wilderness,
in her heat sniffing the wind!
    Who can restrain her lust? (Jeremiah 2:20-25)

U2 jumps from this image of harlotry to the stifling guilt of Judas. The sorrows and guilt of Judas were too much for him to deal with: *I was drowning in my sorrows.* His simultaneous waves of regret and joy come when he finally takes his own life. There, on two separate trees, best friends die. One, however, is resurrected, and he will show the other what the real element of surprise is as he waits until the end of world.

Whereas "Drowning Man" depicts God reaching out to the individual encompassed by a storm, "Until the End of the World" is the drowning man (specifically Judas Iscariot) *reaching out to the one he tried to destroy.* Without reaching a conclusion, Steve Stockman questions whether the song concludes with Judas' salvation or damnation.[25] As was stated at the beginning of this discussion, the song ends with ambiguity, leaving both Judas and the listener wondering about Iscariot's fate.

The first chapter of this book presented some parameters of U2's license for lyrical interpretation. U2's songs are fluid. In Bono's own words, "The songs can completely change their meanings." What I am about to argue is not a total overhaul of "Until the End of the World," but an enhancement to its meaning.

---

[25] Steve Stockman, *Walk On: The Spiritual Journey of U2* (Lake Mary: Relevant Media, 2001) 110.

On the subject of performing live concerts Bono says, "U2 on its own is a very interesting group and all, but U2 with its audience is a *culture*. There are a lot of ideas in and around the band. It's not just the music, and it's only when you get out on the road that that starts to come alive."[26] Juxtaposed with one another, U2's songs can take on greater meanings. While there is no room for this juxtaposition to occur within the studio (except in how an album is constructed), a live concert setting allows U2 the freedom to juggle their songs around.

Placing "Until the End of the World" in the context of U2's live performances since the Zoo TV Tour (1992–93), I believe there is more to be retrieved from this song. In three major concerts—Zoo TV 1992–93, Popmart 1997–98, and Elevation 2001—the song "New Year's Day" (from *War*, 1983) followed "Until the End of the World."[27] Although not all concert songs are strung together for lyrical/thematic coherence, this is a case where surely they are. In a concert setting, the lighting for "Until the End of the World" is somber and sporadic. The confusion of drowning Judas is evident. Once "New Year's Day" begins, however, all lights shine bright, initially blinding the audience. The viewer witnesses a transformation from night into day. The concert shifts its pathos of despair to visible language of amazement, from disorientation to new orientation.

"New Year's Day" was originally written with Poland's Lech Walesa in mind. When the Polish Communist Party incarcerated this leader of Poland's Solidarity Party, U2 wrote of his hopeful reunion with his wife on a New Year's Day.[28] Yet coupled time and again with "Until the End of the World," the song takes on a new meaning, and serves as an interpretive partner for the song it follows. Where "Until the End of the World" ends in disorientation, "New Year's Day" begins with clarity. The title itself is one of new beginnings, a fresh start, and a renewed hope. These lines chase after the turmoil and despondency in which Judas is trapped: *A world in white gets underway . . . I will begin again.*[29]

---

[26] Danny Eccleston, ed. Q4music.com, *U2001 Elevation Tour Book.*
[27] Pimm Jal de la Parra, *U2 Live: A Concert Documentary, Updated Edition* (New York: Omnibus Press, 1997), an exhaustive catalogue of U2's concerts from 1976 to mid 1997.
[28] Stokes, *Into the Heart*, 41.
[29] "New Year's Day," from the album *War.* © 1983 Island Records Ltd.

At the beginning of the chapter I juxtaposed "Drowning Man" with Psalm 13. This was, if you will, suggesting the ringing of certain intertextual echoes. Now consider the possibility of an intratextual relation between "Until the End of the World" and "New Year's Day," an echo suggested by concert performance. Imagine Christ responding with the words of "New Year's Day" to Judas' sad monologue. The clatter of the storm has come to an end. Jesus has calmed the storm and its winds and waves have dissipated. All is quiet on New Year's Day. The darkness and confusion have left. A fresh new world in white gets underway. Where are we? When are we? This is the golden age. Is it really? We are still under a blood-red sky, implying the apocalypse. This is the end of the world. It is called the golden age because *gold is the reason for the wars we wage.* In this time of consummation, Christ responds to Judas, "I have waited until the end of the world for you. I want to be with you again. I will be with you again. Though torn in two we can be one. I will begin again. Behold! I make all things new!" (Revelation 21:5).

"The hope of new creation is the hope of a future for the whole creation which cannot develop out of that creation's inherent potentialities, but can only be given it by a fresh creative act of the transcendent God."[30] Christ has made all things new. When he says, *nothing changes on New Year's Day*, it is good news. This is not a line of resignation to the status quo; it is a hope-filled proclamation. Though wars were once fought over gold, and friendships betrayed for silver, the slate has been wiped clean. This is New Year's Day. And nothing changes on New Year's Day, except now, like Lech Walesa and his wife, the bridegroom and his bride are finally reunited.

In the prologue to his book on Judas, Ray Anderson recounts seeing these words written across the top of a mirror in the men's restroom of a San Francisco restaurant: *JUDAS COME HOME—ALL IS FORGIVEN!* He writes, "If there is a way back home for [Judas], then perhaps there is for us as well—not in retracting our past, but in discovering the love that comes to us from our future."[31]

One final note pertaining to Judas. On its Elevation Tour, U2 has followed "Until the End of the World" with "Stuck in a Moment You

---

[30] Bauckham and Hart, *Hope Against Hope*, 130.
[31] Anderson, *The Gospel According to Judas*, 9, 84.

Can't Get Out Of," a song from their album *ATYCLB*. The song speaks of hope after a long night of despair. Both songs centre on two men who hanged themselves.

Whether they are lost in a postmodern storm or being drowned by guilt and sorrow, U2 asks its audience to stir their imagination and place "a wager on transcendence, on something which lies beyond [them], as yet unseen but . . . real enough."[32] The band makes it possible for this transcendent voice to resound through its songs. If humanity's story is to move into new orientation, "it will only be through the contrivance of the God of the resurrection, the God who is able to bring life out of death."[33] It is such a God who cares deeply for the rights of the poor and offers humanity a vision of a better place. This is the God we meet in the songs found on *The Joshua Tree*.

---

[32] Bauckham and Hart, *Hope Against Hope*, 62.
[33] Ibid., 67.

3
Seeds of Social Justice and Eschatology

"Let those who desire my vindication shout for joy and be glad."
—Psalm 35:27a

*"How long hunger? How long hatred? How long until creation grows up
and the chaos of its precocious, hell-bent adolescence has been discarded?"*
—Bono[1]

Without fully grasping the cutting critique of the "American Dream,"
Americans readily flocked under U2's *Joshua Tree*, making it one of the
most popular albums in rock and roll history. After the success of U2's
previous album *The Unforgettable Fire*, *The Joshua Tree* was released in
1987 at the tail end of "Reagan's America." Unlike its predecessor, *The
Joshua Tree* was an album defined by its musical and lyrical clarity. Following
the Brueggemannian typology discussed in the first chapter, *The Joshua
Tree* begins a sequence of orientation-disorientation-reorientation.
Characterized by Bono and co-producer Brian Eno as an ecstatic and

---

[1] Bono, Introduction to *Selections from the Book of Psalms* (New York: Grove Press, 1999)
xi–xii.

29

gauche album for the eighties, *The Joshua Tree* offered a new and unusual sound for U2's audience. According to Eno, *The Joshua Tree* departed from the direction of rock music at the time in that it was self-consciously spiritual and the band members wore their hearts on their sleeves.[2]

The songs from this album, however, go deeper than the emotional rantings of an over-paid rock group. Stokes remarks that, "As Martin Luther King had emerged as the hero of *The Unforgettable Fire*, now *The Joshua Tree* became a prayer for the dispossessed and for victims of military oppression."[3] In the spirit of such prophets as Isaiah, Jeremiah, and Amos, these songs are an indictment against Reagan's oppressive regime and poems of eschatological hope.

A Poetry of Protest

The songs of *The Joshua Tree* are imaginative works of art protesting the injustices perpetrated by the American government in the eighties. In such a protest imagination is the key. It enables a person to see beyond generally accepted limits and challenge the status quo. It also helps one envision a new reality and construct a different worldview. In other words, imagination empowers humans both to deconstruct a dominant worldview and construct an alternative. Walsh and Middleton define a worldview as a faith commitment that answers the questions of the nature of human purpose (*Who am I?*), the nature of one's universe (*Where am I?*), the basic obstacle obstructing human fulfillment (*What's wrong?*), and the solution of overcoming that obstacle (*What is the remedy?*).[4]

To illustrate, the above questions may be applied to "Reagan's America" in the following manner. *Who am I?* I am an American who wants to live the American dream of financial prosperity. *Where am I?* I live in a democratic, capitalist country. *What's wrong?* The problem is that my country is part of a larger hostile planet full of other countries that are neither democratic nor capitalist. The larger communist countries (Soviet

---

[2] "U2: The Joshua Tree," DVD. © 1999 Eagle Rock Entertainment.
[3] Stokes, *Into the Heart*, 67.
[4] Brian J. Walsh and J. Richard Middleton, *The Transforming Vision: Shaping a Christian Worldview* (Illinois: IVP, 1984) 35.

Union, North Korea, and China) threaten to take over some of the weaker nations, which I happen to exploit in order to carry out my God-given right to an American way of life. *What is the remedy?* The solution to this communist threat is to train and arm the weaker states with whatever means possible (weapons, dictators, media, and the like) to avert the communist threat.

Fearful of "The Domino Effect" in Central America, this is precisely what the United States did. Without regard for human life in Central America, "the United States [conducted] its opposition to communism in such a way that the oppression it [supported] in the Third World [mirrored] the oppression that the communist states [wreaked] on their citizens."[5] The United States poured billions of dollars worth of arms and "economic aid" into Costa Rica, El Salvador, Honduras, and Guatemala with an end result of increased poverty in Central America.

Nicholas Wolterstorff describes this injustice on a global scale. "Those who enjoy a vast range of choice coexist in our world-system with nearly a billion others who live in a state of perpetual poverty, and with hundreds of millions for whom political terror, torture, and tyranny are the ever-present context of their lives—their oppression often being perpetrated or supported by those very governments whose own citizens enjoy great freedom."[6] It is against such injustice that the song "Bullet the Blue Sky" protests. After spending some time in El Salvador observing the realities of a U.S. perpetuated war, Bono began to compose a song that cut into the fabric of American politics and religion. *In the howling wind comes a stinging rain / See it driving nails into souls on the tree of pain / From the firefly, a red orange glow / See the face of fear running scared in the valley below / . . . Outside is America.*[7]

In the days of Amos, the Northern Kingdom of Israel was a rebellious state. Her people had begun to worship their homemade star gods Sikkuth and Kiyyun (Amos 5:26). This false worship was only one of many offences

---

[5] Nicholas Wolterstorff, *Until Justice and Peace Embrace* (Grand Rapids: Eerdmans, 1983) 96.

[6] Ibid., 42.

[7] "Bullet the Blue Sky," from the album *The Joshua Tree.* © 1987 Island Records Ltd. Recommended listening: "Bullet the Blue Sky" (recorded live at the RDS, Dublin, on 28 August 1993) from the single *Stay (Faraway, so close!).* © 1993 Island Records Inc.

committed against Yahweh. The people of Israel had also abandoned those who were close to God's heart: the poor. In *Torah*, God has said of himself:

> For the LORD your God is God of gods and Lord of lords, the great God, mighty and awesome, who is not partial and takes no bribe, who executes justice for the orphan and the widow, and who loves the strangers, providing them food and clothing. You shall also love the stranger, for you were strangers in the land of Egypt. (Deuteronomy 10:17-19)

His words are echoed in the Psalms:

> The LORD opens the eyes of the blind.
> The LORD lifts up those who are bowed down;
> the LORD loves the righteous.
> The LORD watches over the strangers;
> he upholds the orphan and the widow,
> but the way of the wicked he brings to ruin. (Psalm 146:8-9)

Amos appeals to the same law in his indictment against Israel:

> Hear this word, you cows of Bashan who are on Mount Samaria, who oppress the poor, who crush the needy . . . who lie on beds of ivory and lounge on [your] couches . . . you trample on the poor and take from them levies of grain . . . I know how many are your transgressions, and how great are your sins—you who afflict the righteous, who take a bribe, and push aside the needy in the gate . . . You that trample on the needy, and bring to ruin the poor of the land. (Amos 4:1; 6:4; 5:11,12; 8:4)

The very example that God intended to be followed was reversed. The poor were denied justice and propelled deeper into poverty by the levies required of them. The decadence of the northern kingdom, Israel, was mirrored in Judah in the south. Both Jeremiah and Isaiah accused Judah of cheating the poor and, unlike Yahweh, accepting bribes.

> How the faithful city has become a whore!
>   She that was full of justice,

righteousness lodged in her—
> but now murderers!
Your silver has become dross,
> your wine is mixed with water.
Your princes are rebels
> and companions of thieves.
Everyone loves a bribe
> and runs after gifts.
They do not defend the orphan,
> and the widow's cause does not come before them. (Isaiah 1:21-23)

> They have grown fat and sleek.
They know no limits in deeds of wickedness;
> they do not judge with justice
the cause of the orphan, to make it prosper;
> and they do not defend the rights of the needy.
Shall I not punish them for these things? says the LORD,
> and shall I not bring retribution on a nation such as this?
(Jeremiah 5:28)

The prophets have torah-shaped imagination in the service of God. At no point in these indictments do they speak outside of the law. Israel and Judah have no response to offer. Brueggemann offers insight on "spinning" the facts to cover up a crime, relating America to Israel.

> The poet understands the reality and power of the temptation to bury. The poet therefore addresses Israel's sin directly and unflinchingly . . . Israel is immobilized and cannot respond, even in shame. Israel buries the incongruity and loss of wholeness and settles for pretense: "Peace, peace." "America is back." "The market has bottomed out." "It doesn't get any better than this." Israel did not notice. The poet notices though, and cannot remain silent.[8]

In a strikingly similar way, U2 follows the examples of Isaiah, Jeremiah, and Amos. Just as the prophets could not remain silent in the face of

---

[8] Brueggemann, *Finally Comes the Poet*, 16.

Israel's injustices, neither could U2 remain speechless over America's involvement in Central America.

Outside is America

"Bullet the Blue Sky" is more than a political commentary on the forces of democracy waging war against the threat of communism. In a prophetic vein, this song is an indictment against the United States for, in Amos' words, making the bushel smaller and the shekel bigger; cheating with dishonest scales so as to buy the helpless for money and the needy for a pair of shoes (see Amos 8:4-6). Wolterstorff contends: "The United States supports repressive regimes that declare themselves in favor of free enterprise and prove hospitable to American businesses."[9]

The song's final refrain—*Outside is America*—can be heard as the judgment of these crimes. Because America sold out the poor for material gain, God will shut out America. *Outside is America* is a double entendre. Yes, America is outside of the mud hut, with its fighter planes in the sky. Its presence is ominous. But God himself has also shut America outside. As Mary prayed, "He has brought down rulers from their thrones, and has exalted those who were humble. He has filled the hungry with good things; and sent the rich away empty-handed" (Luke 1:52-53; cf. Psalm 107:9). The United States, along with the rest of the western countries has been willing to become fat and sleek at the expense of poorer nations and has gambled with the lives of the vulnerable (*all the colours of a royal flush*); its judgment is to be sent away empty-handed.

The beginning of the song opens the protest. The images of the stinging rain driving nails and the red orange glow from the firefly represent the oppressive military force of America.[10] The driving nails and the red orange glow are bullets and rockets fired at their targets. The first verse also recalls the sacrifice of Christ. Nails being driven into souls on the tree of pain (i.e., the cross) and the face of fear running scared in the valley below are reminding metaphors of Christ's time alone in the Garden of Gethsemane

---

[9] Wolterstorff, *Until Justice and Peace Embrace*, 95. See also Naomi Klein, *No Logo* (Toronto: Knopf Canada, 2000) chapter 9, "The Discarded Factory."

[10] The A/T-17 *Firefly* trainer/light attack jet, TL8 commonly used for advanced pilot training and counterinsurgency operations.

(located in the Kidron Valley) before his arrest. Only this time, it is not Christ who is being sacrificed; it is the orphan and widow of Central America. They too pray to God to take the cup of injustice from them, hoping for a shepherd to guide them safely through the valley of the shadow of death.

The fear-instilling, howling wind becomes a locust wind that greedily consumes everything in its path. The second verse points an accusing finger deep into the heart of America. Did Jacob/America truly overcome the Angel? With Reagan's particular brand of economic and political Constantinianism, could the United States really think to have God in its back pocket, ensuring the country a divine military victory? Was America truly "a city on a hill" as Reagan described her? In truth, no. America's internal state reflects its abhorrent external affairs. The rewards of its foreign policies (*plant a demon seed*) are reaped at home (*you raise a flower of fire*). The flames of fire scorch the land through white supremacist groups such as the Ku Klux Klan (*see them burning crosses, see the flames, higher and higher*).

The song continues to interweave politics and religion by hinting culpability at American televangelists. The *suit and tie with a face red like a rose on a thorn bush* is a reference to Jerry Falwell and his wealthy televangelist contemporaries.[11] On its live album *Rattle and Hum*, U2 follows a mocking Jimmy Hendrix guitar version of "The Star Spangled Banner" with "Bullet the Blue Sky." As the song concludes, Bono rails: *I can't tell the difference between ABC News, Hill Street Blues, and a preacher on The Old Time Gospel Hour, stealing money from the sick and the old. Well the God I believe in isn't short of cash, mister. And I feel a long way from the fields of San Salvador.*[12]

The contrast between a fat and sleek preacher thumbing through a roll of bills and shelterless widows and orphans evokes a rage in the heart of U2 that parallels these thoughts from Wolterstorff:

> I want to say, as emphatically as I can, that our concern with poverty is not an issue of generosity but of rights. If a rich man knows of someone who is starving and has the power to help that person but chooses not

---

[11] Stokes, *Into the Heart*, 68.
[12] "Bullet the Blue Sky," from the album *Rattle and Hum*. © 1988 Island Records Ltd.

to do so, then he violates the starving person's rights as surely and reprehensibly as if he had physically assaulted the sufferer.[13]

Jeremiah had to contend with the religious establishment as well. Having fooled themselves into believing their own self-righteous lies, the Temple authorities put their confidence in a structural edifice instead of the living God. Similarly, the politician and the preacher make the same fatal mistake by putting their trust in America and her dollar. Through Jeremiah, Yahweh responded:

Here you are, trusting in deceptive words to no avail. Will you steal, murder, commit adultery, swear falsely, make offerings to Baal, and go after other gods that you have not known, and then come and stand before me in this house, which is called by my name, and say, "We are safe!"—only to go on doing all these abominations? (Jeremiah 7:8-10)

The Joshua Tree concludes with the horrific outcome of America's foreign policy in the song, "Mothers of the Disappeared." The song laments the hundreds of students who opposed the military regimes of Central America and Argentina in the seventies and eighties. They had been arrested and never heard of again. In Argentina, they became known as "the disappeared."[14] Inspired by their stories and their mothers who formed the organization "Mothers of the Disappeared," U2 wrote: *Midnight, our sons and daughters / were cut down and taken from us / Hear their heartbeat . . . / We hear their heartbeat / in the trees.*[15] The howling wind and stinging rain of "Bullet the Blue Sky" serve as painful reminders of lost loved ones. The "tree of pain" depicts the mother's anguish as her sons stand naked and helpless in her mind. Now, through the walls, the cries of her daughters clash with the city groan. The stretched out night with a black and blue sky only reminds the mother of her tortured children. The song begins at midnight but never quite makes it to the morning (see Psalm 130:5-6). What these mothers want, what they are deprived of, what they deserve, is

[13] Nicholas Wolterstorff, *Until Justice and Peace Embrace*, 82.
[14] Stokes, *Into the Heart*, 77.
[15] "Mothers of the Disappeared," from the album *The Joshua Tree*. © 1987 Island Records Ltd.

justice. Israel's God-haunted prophets, along with the poor and oppressed, were also preoccupied with justice. "Israel's daily appetite is that the world should be equitable. Israel's very existence as a historical community is dependent and derived from Yahweh's initial, even primordial, preoccupation with justice."[16] In a letter to North American Christians, thirteen Christians from Latin America wrote about their deprivation of justice.

> Your precious "American Way of Life"—the opulence of your magnates,
> your economic and military dominion—feeds in no small proportion
> on the blood that gushes, according to one of our most brilliant essayists,
> "from the open veins of Latin America."[17]

Justice, contends Wolterstorff, is a right that belongs to every human being.[18] In the songs described above, U2 depict the cruel injustices common to Central America, which are, ironically, caused by America, a land known for its justice.

Where Brueggemann would argue that God has "shaped and settled the focus of the Bible on the issue of justice," Wolterstorff would take it a step further.[19] Wolterstorff agrees on the great importance of justice, but argues that there is still something greater yet. It is a state where the human being dwells in peace in all her relationships (e.g., with God, self, others, and nature). It is *shalom*.[20]

Eschatological Birth Pangs

Alongside its indictment for the failure of justice, *The Joshua Tree* yields songs that yearn for the Consummation. "Eschatology," argue Bauckham and Hart, "is above all a source of hope and liberation, and is addressed, therefore, to those who, in one way or another, find themselves in the grip of hopelessness, slavery or oppression."[21] There is a marked difference

---

[16] Brueggemann, *The Psalms and the Life of Faith*, 61.
[17] Wolterstorff, *Until Justice and Peace Embrace*, 97–98.
[18] Ibid., 71.
[19] Brueggemann, *The Psalms and the Life of Faith*, 61.
[20] Wolterstorff, *Until Justice and Peace Embrace*, 69.
[21] Bauckham and Hart, *Hope Against Hope*, 193.

between eschatological hope and eschatological escapism. The escapism can be seen in such forms as the Left Behind series and other sensionalistic books and movies rising from a growing Christian evangelical subculture. This hope, however, is not founded in a special revelation of "end-time" events, but in a well-founded trust that Yahweh will bring this world and its history to their proper end, transforming creation into something wholly new and unprecedented.[22]

We live in a world where the majority of human beings are left abandoned in absolute poverty, where human rights are a commodity for the privileged few, and where for the most part, one third of the world is oblivious to the injustices of the other two thirds.[23] Despite the odds against the poor, there is hope and ultimate liberation. God is on the side of the poor. That is Wolterstorff's conclusion. He writes,

> It is against [God's] will that there be a society in which some are poor; in his perfected Kingdom there will be none at all. It is even more against his will that there be a society in which some are poor while others are rich. When that happens, then he is on the side of the poor, for it is they, he says, who are being wronged.[24]

Yet if this is true, and Yahweh does contend for the poor, why does a world with so much poverty exist? Though the songs we are about to discuss do not answer the questions of theodicy, they do long for an equal society, and a time when poverty and injustice will be eradicated.

Two years before the release of *The Joshua Tree*, Bono and his wife Alison spent six weeks working at an orphanage in Wello, Ethiopia. Bono recalls, "You'd walk out of your tent, and you'd count bodies of dead and abandoned children. Or worse, the father of a child would walk up to you and try to give you his living child and say, 'You take it, because if this is your child, it won't die.'"[25] Bono and Ali placed themselves in a

---

[22] Ibid., 79.
[23] Wolterstorff, *Until Justice and Peace Embrace*, 74, 188. Absolute poverty is defined as "a condition of life so characterized by malnutrition, illiteracy, disease, squalid surroundings, high infant mortality and low life expectancy as to be beneath any reasonable definition of human decency."
[24] Ibid., 76. Cf. Isaiah 3:13-15, 10:1-2.
[25] Tyrangiel, "Bono's Mission," 63.

circumstance where they were forced to ask the introspective question of how one ought to live in light of this poverty. As soon as that question is asked, says Goldmann, "the reply is already implicit: by situating one's life inside an eschatological or historical whole in which it inserts itself by faith."[26] With a firsthand experience of the world's inequity, Bono was supplied with the raw fodder required for composing poetry situated inside an eschatological whole.

The remainder of this chapter will analyze two of *The Joshua Tree's* most popular songs, "Where the Streets Have No Name" and "I Still Haven't Found What I'm Looking For." These two poems, with their malaise and longing, cling to the hope that history is moving towards a culmination. Although pain and suffering mark today, an endless tomorrow is anticipated full of peace and justice. The lyrics of "Where the Streets Have No Name" begin the album: *I want to run / I want to hide / I want to tear down the walls / That hold me inside / I want to reach out / And touch the flame / Where the streets have no name.*[27]

Looking back at these lyrics, Bono articulates the sentiment he tried to convey at the time:

> Do you want to go on a journey to somewhere that none of us have ever been before, to that place where you forget yourself, and who you are, and where you can imagine something better? It's a spine-chilling moment for you as a singer, and anyone in the audience. But it comes out on *The Joshua Tree*, as 'I want to run, I want to hide, I want to tear down these walls that hold me inside.' That is so sophomoric. But that is the way it came out.[28]

As sophomoric as Bono may think it sounds, in a nutshell, "Where the Streets Have No Name" is a longing for the Kingdom of God. The song anticipates a time and a place of equality for all of humanity. It is an

---

[26] Lucien Goldmann, *The Hidden God: A Study of Tragic Vision in the "Pensées" of Pascal and the Tragedies of Racine*, trans. Philip Thody (New York: Humanities Press, 1964) 264.
[27] "Where the Streets Have No Name," from the album *The Joshua Tree*. © 1987 Island Records Ltd. Recommended listening: "Where the Streets Have No Name" (live from Boston, 6 June 2001) from the single *Walk On.* " 2001 Universal Music International.
[28] Erik Philbrook, "Keeping the Peace," *Playback*, October 2001.

anthem for the dispossessed. It is the ongoing response to a constricting world whose walls are slowly closing in.

The song also evokes the pathos of liberation. To run, hide, and tear down are all verbs used in an act of escape. But escape to where exactly? The setting of the song sets the tone for the rest of *The Joshua Tree*. We are in the desert. It could be the sun-scorched soil of Ethiopia or the American wasteland where we *Dream beneath a desert sky / The rivers run / But soon run dry / We need new dreams tonight.*[29]

Eventually, the desert shrivels all resources. It is a place of cruel elements. With its harsh winds it beats and tramples its victims, choking their imagination with its dust clouds and offering no shelter from acid rains. The desert is a place where an imperfect love, marred by sin, turns to rust. The efforts of building relationships or peace talks (e.g., Northern Ireland) are delusional. The desert's inhabitants become trapped in this futile exercise of rebuilding what the desert only burns down.

"Where the Streets Have No Name" should not be interpreted as the desert. It is precisely the opposite. "Where the Streets Have No Name" is a place without prejudice and hatred. The title of the song does not refer to a region of ambiguity or postal confusion. Rather, the song title implies a place of equality. Without names, all streets are equal; without labels of prejudice, race, economic status, and so forth, all people are equal. We read this in a familiar part of Isaiah:

> Every valley shall be lifted up,
>   and every mountain and hill be made low;
> the uneven ground shall become level,
>   and the rough places a plain.
>
> Then the glory of the LORD shall be revealed,
>   and all people shall see it together,
> for the mouth of the LORD has spoken. (Isaiah 40:4-5)

Isaiah introduces a concept of "leveling" or equalizing. He speaks of a time when God himself arrives. And on that day, he will change the

---

[29] "In God's Country," from the album *The Joshua Tree*. © 1987 Island Records Ltd.

landscape of humanity, providing us with a place where we stand together, shoulder to shoulder.

This is a place above the grueling desert, high on a desert plain.[30] Where the streets have no name is a place where the suffocating dust cloud has vanished without a trace and the warm sunlight makes its way to the face of every citizen. This is an area of shelter and community. Individualism and selfishness are banned from this city. When I go there, I do not go alone, I go there with you. Community, safety, equality, and justice: these words help define this region of the imagination. The prophet Isaiah writes,

> When the Lord has washed away the filth of the daughters of Zion, and purged the bloodshed of Jerusalem from her midst, by the spirit of judgment and the spirit of burning, then the LORD will create over the whole area of Mount Zion and over her assemblies a cloud by day, even smoke, and the brightness of a flaming fire by night; for over all the glory will be a canopy. And there will be a shelter to give shade from the heat by day, and refuge and protection from the storm and the rain. (Isaiah 4:4-6)

Evoking memories of the exodus and the wilderness wanderings, Isaiah uses ordinary language to share a vision of the extraordinary and the unexplainable. Bono's juvenile, ecstatic (and sometimes elusive) utterances are similar metaphors employed to convey a sense of hope in the midst of despair.

Yet there is more to this place of hope than community, safety, equality, and justice. *Shalom* completes a Kingdom where the streets have no name. "In *shalom* each person enjoys justice, enjoys his or her rights. There is no *shalom* without justice. But *shalom* goes beyond justice. *Shalom* is the human being dwelling at peace in all his or her relationships: with God, with self, with fellows, with nature."[31] All of creation will share in this harmony. Again Isaiah employs common language to construe the unsayable.[32]

---

[30] Cf. Isaiah 58:12 "Your ancient ruins shall be rebuilt; you shall raise up the foundations of many generations; you shall be called the repairer of the breach, the restorer of streets to live in."

[31] Wolterstorff, *Until Justice and Peace Embrace*, 69.

[32] Bauckham & Hart offer an excellent discussion on "Ambiguous Vision: Hope, Imagination and the Rhetoric of the Unsayable," 72–108.

And the wolf will dwell with the lamb,
>   and the leopard will lie down with the kid,
and the calf and the young lion and the fatling together;
>   and a little boy will lead them.
Also the cow and the bear will graze;
>   their young will lie down together;
>   and the lion will eat straw like the ox.
And the nursing child will play by the hole of the cobra,
>   and the weaned child will put his hand on the
>   viper's den. (Isaiah 11:6-8)

Throughout the book of Isaiah, Yahweh has woven glimpses of *shalom*. This would include the portion Jesus read from in Nazareth. Jesus chooses such an Isaian prophecy of *shalom* to inaugurate his ministry in the synagogue of Nazareth:

"The Spirit of the Lord is upon me,
because he has anointed me
to bring good news to the poor.
He has sent me to proclaim
release to the captives
and recovery of sight to the blind,
to let the oppressed go free,
to proclaim the year of the Lord's favor."
And he rolled up the scroll, gave it back to the attendant,
and sat down.
The eyes of all in the synagogue were fixed on him
(Luke 4:18-20; see Isaiah 61:1-3)

Wolterstorff comments on this passage: "Isaiah was speaking of the day of shalom. In shalom there are no blind . . . To limp is to fall short of shalom. To be impoverished is to fall short of shalom. *That* is what is wrong with poverty. God is committed to shalom. Jesus came to bring shalom. In shalom there is no poverty."[33] Through Christ, *shalom* has

---

[33] Wolterstorff, *Until Justice and Peace Embrace*, 77.

been inaugurated. Yet its full effects have not been completely realized. Only hints of *shalom* can be detected in the present.

Bauckham and Hart's discussion of hope can be applied to *shalom* as well. Humanity is on "a quest for something more, something better, than the present affords."[34] Herein lies the ache of "I Still Haven't Found What I'm Looking For." Contrary to the Evangelical church's interpretation of U2 turning its back on God, this song is sung on a journey for something greater. I remember listening to the ramblings of preachers sermonizing over the contempt of this song. "How could a Christian who is in relationship with God, claim that he still hasn't found what he's looking for?" This was the popular critique of the contemptuous refrain. To this day, in discussions and talks concerning God and U2, parishioners and university students alike pose the same question. U2 is not expressing their dissatisfaction with salvation; they are, along with the prophets, yearning for the day of *shalom*. They are, along with the apostle Paul, "forgetting what lies behind and straining forward to what lies ahead" (Philippians 3:12). *I have climbed the highest mountains / I have run through the fields / Only to be with you.*[35]

The voice in "I Still Haven't Found What I'm Looking For" is searching for a place "Where the Streets Have No Name." This person has traversed the desert wilderness and the cityscape in search of *shalom*. Encountering a spectrum of human experiences, the singer's longing is never quite fulfilled.

This song is a lament addressed to Christ. In light of the injustices in "Bullet the Blue Sky" and "Mothers of the Disappeared," and the ideal state where the streets have no name, "I Still Haven't Found What I'm Looking For" is Bono's complaint to Christ. Brueggemann writes, "the laments show clearly that *biblical faith, as it faces life fully, is uncompromisingly and unembarrassedly dialogic.* Israel and Israelites in their hurt have to do with God, and God has to do with them. The laments are addressed to someone! . . . Nowhere but with God does Israel vent its greatest doubt, its bitterest resentments, its deepest anger."[36] The song

---

[34] Bauckham and Hart, *Hope Against Hope*, 72.

[35] "I Still Haven't Found What I'm Looking For," from the album *The Joshua Tree*. © 1987 Island Records Ltd. Recommended listening: "I Still Haven't Found What I'm Looking For," from the album *Rattle and Hum*. © 1988 Island Records Ltd.

[36] Brueggemann, *The Psalms and the Life of Faith*, 68.

reiterates the question of "40," *How long to sing this song?* How long must the singer continue the quest before finally finding what he is looking for? The song reveals a statement of faith in the fourth stanza: *I believe in the Kingdom Come / Then all the colours will bleed into one / But yes I'm still running / You broke the bonds / You loosed the chains / You carried the cross / And my shame.*

Bono believes in *shalom*. The Kingdom of God will be fully realized when all the colours of race and flag will bleed into one. But it has not yet arrived. And it is in this "not yet" that this song—and all of Christian faith—must live. Despite his deep appreciation for redemption, Bono is not satisfied (*But I still haven't found what I'm looking for*). Rather than a spirituality of self-satisfied "arrival," this is a spirituality that still sojourns in the wilderness. There is more of *shalom* to come and the song asks God when that will be. This song is not an exception of the Christian life; rather, Bauckham and Hart point out that

> Christianity is a faith which is essentially forward looking and forward moving, orientated towards and living now ever in the light cast backwards by God's promised future . . . It transcends the limits of any and every particular human present, looking beyond the often dark and unbearable experiences of the here and now, refusing to accept the suffering, injustice, lack and loss which characterize so much of life, and reaching not upwards to a 'spiritual' escape hatch from this world, but forwards to a time when such things will cease, and the pain and loss be redeemed and refashioned into something good and enduring.[37]

"I Still Haven't Found What I'm Looking For" and "Where the Streets Have No Name" look forward and move toward the light of God's promised future. They are not songs of escapism; rather, they anticipate the day of *shalom*'s full incursion onto creation, where there will be no sorrow and no shame.

To revisit Brueggemann for a moment, I have interpreted *The Joshua Tree* as an album of orientation. It is a focussed record where both the artists and audience hold to honesty and sincerity. There is also an insatiable yearning for *shalom* reflected on this album. That longing will never be

---

[37] Bauckham and Hart, *Hope Against Hope*, 82.

satisfied in the state of orientation. As mentioned earlier, the place of orientation is a shallow, almost naïve one. Wallowing along the shoreline cannot dissipate the malaise that hangs in the air. An unexpected, traumatic shift must occur to assuage the restlessness expressed in the album. For U2, that traumatic shift occurred in the ensuing decade (1989–99). Masked with a feigned megalomania, the band would explore the bleak desert landscape that they discovered on *The Joshua Tree*, sending their audience into a constructed disorientation. The underlying lack of *shalom* that exists in apparent orientation must be exposed and resolved. For U2, the deeper, dark waters were made up of cynicism, longing, and satire. The following chapter will join U2 for a decade of pomp, decadence, and personal demons, revealed in the triadic collection of *Achtung Baby*, *Zooropa*, and *Pop*.

4

The Babylonian State of Zooropa

*"We do not measure a culture by its output of undisguised trivialities
but by what it claims as significant."*
—Neil Postman[1]

*"Rock & roll music—the noisier the better—is still my alarm clock.
It still keeps me awake. It's a hymn to the numbness,
a reasonable response to the way we live."*
—Bono[2]

*"I fall down, Heaven won't help me . . .
I'm having trouble just finding my soul in this town"*
—Noel Gallagher[3]

---

[1] Neil Postman, *Amusing Ourselves to Death: Public Discourse in the Age of Show Business*
(New York: Penguin, 1985) 16.
[2] David Fricke, "U2 Finds What It's Looking For," *Rolling Stone*, 1 October 1992,
U2: The Rolling Stone Files (New York: Hyperion, 1994) 188.
[3] Noel Gallagher, "Part of the Queue," from the album *Don't Believe the Truth*. © 2005
Sony/ATV Music Publishing UK Ltd. / Oasis Music.

The foreboding desert landscape of *The Joshua Tree* provides the subject matter for U2's next three albums. The trilogy of *Achtung Baby*, *Zooropa*, and *Pop* uses wide brushes and brilliant colours to describe the drab, consumerist wasteland of Western culture. This trilogy takes U2's listeners from an oriented world in which laments were blatant and obvious, to a place of deep disorientation where laments are disguised with humour and irony.

As was mentioned in the previous chapter, *The Joshua Tree* was replete with songs that lamented issues of social injustice and global terror that were inextricably linked to America's foreign policy. *Achtung Baby* (1991) and its tour child *Zooropa* (1993) were produced during the Gulf War. Wanting to address the anesthetized televised reporting so common on CNN and similar Western broadcasting networks, Bono shares his dilemma on how to effectively express his ideas.

> I realized I couldn't write songs about it. Everything we'd learned in the last ten years meant nothing in the face of this, that we could talk so coldly about flesh being burned off people's bodies. Humor was the only response. I knew we had to find different ways of saying the same thing. Writing and approaching this head-on just would not work.[4]

It comes as no surprise, then, to hear Bono's distorted voice sing the opening lines of "Zoo Station," *Achtung Baby*'s first track: *I'm ready / Ready for the laughing gas / I'm ready / Ready for what's next.*[5] The listener is forewarned. This may not be the time for laughing, but if laughter is the only way to address the issues, then laugh you will. The listener is transported to a train station (Zoo Station to be precise) in the middle of nowhere, where:

---

[4] David Fricke, "U2 Finds What It's Looking For," *Rolling Stone*, 1 October 1992, *U2: The Rolling Stone Files* (New York: Hyperion, 1994) 185. Kenneth J. Gergen agrees with Bono. "Those working within the postmodern idiom have a common rejoinder—essentially an invitation to play. For once it is realized that all attempts to 'tell the truth,' to be wise, insightful, intelligent, or profound, are constructions of language . . . then it becomes very difficult to make a deeply serious investment in such tellings . . . the favored option for many is to indulge in the communal constructions, but with humor, irony, and humility." *The Saturated Self: Dilemmas of Identity in Contemporary Life* (New York: Basic Books, 1991) 137.
[5] "Zoo Station," from the album *Achtung Baby*. © 1991 Island Records Ltd.

Time is a train / Makes the future the past / Leaves you standing in the station / Your face pressed up against the glass.[6] With warnings of whiplash, *Achtung Baby* is a dizzying collection of sounds whose metaphors could be speaking of either women or God.[7] Without delving too far into the next chapter, the contrast of opening songs on the albums *Achtung Baby* and *ATYCLB* is striking. *Achtung Baby*'s departure point is a train station, ready to send its listener upon a train odyssey that is destined for derailment, whereas *ATYCLB* begins at an airport with limitless possibilities for elevation. *Achtung Baby* concludes with the hymnic vibrations of a pipe organ. Just when the journey appears to reach its end, "Love is Blindness" becomes an interpretive bridge into the land of Zooropa. *Love is blindness / I don't want to see / Won't you wrap the night / Around me.*[8] The mournful character of the music is reminiscent of a funeral procession. Given its references to blindness and night, the metaphor of "tunnel" rather than "bridge" is more appropriate for this song. It could be interpreted as the end of modernity. The candle of the Enlightenment has been blown out. All we are left with is a postmodern darkness. Steinar Kvale describes postmodern thought as "characterized by a loss of belief in an objective world and an incredulity towards meta-narratives of legitimation. With a delegitimation of global systems of thought, there is no foundation to secure a universal and objective *reality*."[9] According to "Love is Blindness," *love* is the secure reality whose foundation is crumbling. Though interwoven with sexual innuendo (*thread ripping, the knot slipping, in a parked car, take the money / honey*) this concluding song depicts the hopelessness of a loveless world.

It ultimately climaxes by entertaining the notion of suicide (*A little death / Without mourning / . . . And no warning / . . . a dangerous idea / That almost makes sense*). The singer wants to be enveloped by the night. He wants to be blinded by anything that will offer to heal his hurt, even if that something is death (*Won't you wrap the night / Around me*).

Riding through the seemingly endless dreadful tunnel of night, U2's train emerges in *a city without a soul, under an atomic sky, where the ground won't turn, and the rain it burns.*[10] In this city, reduced to machinery, *Love*

---

[6] Ibid.

[7] Stockman, *Walk On*, 109.

[8] "Love is Blindness," from the album *Achtung Baby*. © 1991 Island Records Ltd.

[9] Walter Truett Anderson, ed., *The Truth About the Truth*, 19.

[10] "The Wanderer," from the album *Zooropa*. © 1993 Polygram International Music BV.

is clockworks / And cold steel. This city robs its citizens of any semblance of community. Identity is comprised of slogans. This city is the opposite of "Where the Streets Have No Name." Instead of hope, there is consumerism. Instead of shalom, there is conformity. Instead of life, there is only numbness. Welcome to a new and improved Babylon. Welcome to a "world possessed . . . a world overrun by irrationality, by terror-crazed ideologies and by the demonic."[11] Welcome to the wasteland called Zooropa.

Bono, Brueggemann, and Babylon

Anthony DeCurtis calls *Zooropa* "a daring, imaginative coda to *Achtung Baby*. It is varied and vigorously experimented, but its charged mood of giddy anarchy suffused with barely suppressed dread provides a compelling, unifying thread."[12] Israel's exilic Babylon is U2's Zooropa. Brueggemann offers keen insights on Babylon and exile. He writes that, "The prophet must speak not only about the abandonment of Israel by its God but about the specificity of Babylon."[13] U2 puts its finger on "Babylon," identifying this empire in the songs of *Zooropa* and *Pop*. Brueggemann also notes that, "Exile did not lead Jews in the Old Testament to abandon faith or to settle for abdicating despair, nor to retreat to privatistic religion. On the contrary, exile evoked the most brilliant literature and the most daring theological articulation in the Old Testament."[14] It is true that the Babylonian exile evoked much of Israel's brilliant literature. Yet what Brueggemann fails to address is that this same literature was meant to inspire those who acquiesced to Babylon's empire. The exile *did* lead Jews in the Old Testament to abandon faith. This great exilic literature, argue Bauckham and Hart, was aimed at those who found themselves "in the grip of hopelessness, slavery or oppression . . . It [was] directly political in nature, designed to shape the actions of the oppressed by capturing their

---

[11] Bob Goudzwaard, *Idols of Our Time* (Iowa: Dordt College Press, 1981) 9.
[12] Anthony DeCurtis, "*Zooropa* Album Review: *Zooropa* Mon Amour," *Rolling Stone*, August 5, 1993, *U2: The Rolling Stone Files* (New York: Hyperion, 1994) 202.
[13] Brueggemann, *The Prophetic Imagination*, 67.
[14] Ibid., *Cadences of Home: Preaching Among Exiles* (Louisville: WJK Press, 1997) 3.

imaginations and offering a transforming vision of God's future."[15] Walsh concurs with their explanation. Referring to the idolatrous modern worldview he states that

> this is the worldview that captivates the *imagination* of our society . . .
> We live in Babylon. Babylonian definitions of reality, Babylonian patterns
> of life, Babylonian views of labour and Babylonian economic structures
> dominate our waking, and our sleeping. And, like the exiled Jews, we
> find it very tempting to think that all of this is normal. This is the way
> life basically should be.[16]

Our imagination is the prize for competing empires: Babylon versus the Kingdom of God. Just as Isaiah and Jeremiah struggled to liberate the imagination of their people by naming and unmasking Babylon, in a similar fashion, U2 takes on the challenge of naming and unmasking Zooropa. Perhaps by naming the empire, the band can help people recognize it for what it is: a controlling system that excels in the numbing of its slaves. Walsh categorizes three of Babylon's demi-gods used to keep the populace paralyzed. They are Scientism, Technicism, and Economism.[17] U2 identifies this triad in the song "Zooropa." The subway has come to a grinding halt. Last stop: Dead-end Zooropa.[18]

Musically, as well as thematically, "Zooropa" is the anti-matter of "Where the Streets Have No Name." The song opens with background noise "courtesy of the advertising world."[19] If one listens carefully, she can also hear the voice of George Herbert Walker Bush amidst the cacophony of voices saying, "Peace talks." Yet peace has nothing to do with "Zooropa." "Where the Streets Have No Name" is about the Kingdom of God. It is about eventual fulfillment and completion. It is about certainty, hope, and shalom. "Zooropa," on the other hand, offers no fulfillment, no certainty, no hope, no compass, no map, no religion. Zooropa is hell on

---

[15] Bauckham & Hart, 193.

[16] Brian Walsh, *Subversive Christianity* (Seattle: Alta Vista College Press, 1994) 16, 17.

[17] Ibid., 16. See also Walsh & Middleton, *The Transforming Vision*, 131–46.

[18] "Zooropa," from the album *Zooropa*. © 1993 Polygram International Music BV.

[19] Listed in the credits of "Zooropa." DeCurtis describes: "As the song opens, a stately piano figure, beautiful and foreboding, underlies indecipherable, static-stricken signals from the information-age inferno of Zoo TV," 203.

earth. The song only gives its listeners an empty shell of advertising slogans in answer to those repetitive haunting questions: What do you want? *(Qu'est-ce que tu veux?)* What are you afraid of? *(De quoi as-tu peur?)*. Whatever you want, whatever you are afraid of, Zooropa's demi-gods of scientism, technicism, and economism are ready to accommodate. U2 weaves Zooropa's creed by borrowing slogans from various corporations:

- *Vorsprung durch Technik* ("Advancement through technology," Audi)
- Be all that you can be (U.S. Army)
- Be a winner (the lotteries)
- Eat to get slimmer (Slimfast)
- A bluer kind of white (Persil/Daz)
- We're mild and green, and squeaky clean (Fairy Liquid Mild Green)
- Better by design (Toshiba)
- Fly the friendly skies (United Airlines)
- Through appliance of science (Zanussi)
- We've got that ring of confidence (Colgate)[20]

In a critique of modernity, Bob Goudzwaard comments on the subject of idolatry: "How strange that our solutions—economic growth, technological development, the advance of the applied sciences and the expansion of the state—have hardened our problems! Our solutions have turned against us."[21] Indeed! These gods—Scientism, Technicism, and Economism—have left our culture droning: *I feel numb / Too much is not enough / Gimme some more.*[22] Gergen defines the postmodern condition as being

> marked by a plurality of voices vying for the right to reality—to be accepted as legitimate expressions of the true and the good. As the voices expand in power and presence, all that seemed proper, right-minded, and well understood is subverted.[23]

With their "ridiculous voices" the gods sell their hollow wares and in turn strip their buyers of direction, purpose, boundaries and a sense of God

---

[20] These slogans were paired with their corporations at www.@u2.com.
[21] Goudzwaard, *Idols of Our Time*, 12.
[22] "Numb," from the album *Zooropa*. © 1993 Polygram International Music BV.
[23] Gergen, *The Saturated Self*, 7.

(*And I have no compass / And I have no map / And I have no reasons / No reasons to get back / And I have no religion / And I don't know what's what / And I don't know the limit / The limit of what we got*).

Modernity, however, is not the only culprit. The postmodern response to this directionless crisis is just as great a lie as its modern sister's. Postmodernity allows no room for grand stories and large visions (*no particular place names / no particular song*) opening the door for individuals to create their own reality (*uncertainty . . . can be a guiding light / . . . She's gonna dream up the world she wants to live in / She's gonna dream out loud*). Without a grand story to retain the stability of the community and the individual, our culture's "ideal of authenticity frays about the edges," as it drifts aimlessly on a horizonless ocean.[24] U2 capture this anchorless feeling in the refrains of one of their more ambiguous songs titled "Lemon." *I feel like I'm holding onto nothing / . . . / And I feel like I'm drifting, drifting, drifting from the shore.*[25]

Imagination is precisely what has been stolen from our culture. The loss of our imagination has left us with no feeling, except for an insatiable desire to consume. "Give me some more. Too much is not enough." This is Zooropa. It is a spectacle without substance. It is a bright town without warmth (*it's cold outside but brightly lit*). Yet a faint trace of hope lies in the song. "Lemon" speaks of imagination as a destination. While adrift on the sea, the lost come to realize that there is a destination. Could it be that, even in the land of Zooropa, someone is singing a song of hope? There is a glimmer of hope that one day imagination will be restored.

Wandering through Zooropa

Until that time of restoration, however, the people of Zooropa are left wandering. Unlike "I Still Haven't Found What I'm Looking For," where the eschatological yearning for shalom is distinct, "The Wanderer" acts as *Zooropa's* apathetic bookend, providing another facet of Zooropa. Whereas the person in "I Still Haven't Found What I'm Looking For" is actively searching for the Kingdom of God, "The Wanderer" moves about aimlessly. *Zooropa's* final song continues the journey into the emptiness of Babylon.

---

[24] Ibid., 150.
[25] "Lemon," from the album *Zooropa*. © 1993 Polygram International Music BV.

I went out walking under an atomic sky / Where the ground won't turn / And the rain it burns / Like the tears when I said goodbye.[26]

Zooropa may be a city with streets paved with gold, but it is far from being a utopia. Zooropa is the deconstruction of utopia. It is a dystopia.[27] This is a city, as Middleton and Walsh would describe, "in the depths of a cultural winter."[28] Zooropa is a graveyard. It is an infrastructure without a soul. Nothing grows in this city because the burning rain that falls from an atomic sky scorches the ground, rendering it untillable. All imagination has been burned away, and the Wanderer goes out with nothing, nothing but the thought of her. "She's imagination." The Wanderer is the one who is "drifting, drifting, drifting from the shore" in "Lemon." He wants to find her, but the nature of his nameless identity (*looking for my own name*) won't allow it. A sojourner has a destination. A wanderer is aimless.

The Wanderer goes out with nothing except a divine void begging to be filled. The song intersects well with U2's "Mofo." As if looking back on a fruitless stroll through a shopping mall, the voice in "Mofo" laments: *lookin' for to save my save my soul / lookin' in the places where no flowers grow / lookin' for to fill that GOD shaped hole.*[29] What does the Wanderer attempt to fill this God-shaped hole with? Like the prodigal son, he traipses about in search of as much tangible pleasure as possible. The song concludes with the Wanderer never finding that "one good man whose spirit will not bend or break." Although he longs for a messiah, he is powerless to break out of Zooropa.[30] Yet the very mentioning of this God-man suggests that he does exist. The tension of this silent Messiah is carried over to the

---

[26] "The Wanderer," from the album *Zooropa*. © 1993 Polygram International Music BV.
[27] Bauckham & Hart write of how Antichrist "portrays the common future of all human history, not as paradise at last achieved, but as the tower of Babel finally completed, the globalization of humanity's most evil and idolatrous tendencies. If the millennium is the Christian tradition's utopia, the reign of Antichrist is its dystopia. Utopia cannot be the product of history, only of God's redemption of history," 115. Cf. Middleton & Walsh (15–27) on constructing Babel.
[28] Middleton & Walsh, *Truth is Stranger Than it Used to Be*, 25.
[29] "Mofo," from the album *Pop*. © 1997 Polygram International Music BV.
[30] Steve Turner, *Hungry for Heaven: Rock 'n' Roll & the Search for Redemption*, (Downers Grove, Illinois: IVP, 1995) 185. Regarding "The Wanderer," the author quotes Bono. "The song is definitely the antidote to the Zooropa manifesto of uncertainty . . . Even if the album begins with 'I don't have a compass / I don't have a map,' this track gives one possible solution." I argue against this optimistic interpretation.

song "Wake Up Dead Man" on U2's subsequent album, *Pop*. The aggravating alarm that closes the album signals a new chapter. Bauckham and Hart wonder,

> Can we manage with mere disillusioned pragmatism or hedonism? Can we live in the present without meaningful hope for the future? Are we content to celebrate the millennium as a postmodern game, enjoying the party as though there were no tomorrow?[31]

But there is a tomorrow. It is time to wake up and face a new day. When the curtains are pulled back, though, the sky is still red. The earth is still scorched. This is still Zooropa. Nothing has changed. Last night's party is over and it is time to deal with the hangover.

The End of a Postmodern Party

Stockman cites Salman Rushdie recalling a meal at Bono's home in Killiney, south Dublin, when German film director Wim Wenders "announced that artists must no longer use irony. Plain speaking, he argued, was necessary now. Communication should be direct, and anything that might create confusion should be eschewed."[32] Not heeding their friend's new insight, U2 decided to take their music to a deeper level of disorientation on their next album, *Pop*.

Zooropa's presence is ominous on this album. *Pop* is described by Irish journalist Stuart Baillie as "watching the world dancing and shagging and shopping and suggesting that it is ultimately joyless."[33] Bono himself referred to *Pop* as "a party for two songs, and then it's the hangover."[34] Apparently "too much" is getting to be more than enough. Zooropa's self-indulgent, postmodern party is becoming somewhat wearisome, and the Wanderer needs a way out.

Unfortunately, the Wanderer is alone. Unlike the community in "Where the Streets Have No Name," Zooropa has no community. There

[31] Bauckham & Hart, *Hope Against Hope*, 9.
[32] Stockman, *Walk On*, 165.
[33] Ibid., 139.
[34] Heath, "U2: Band of the Year," 41.

is only solitude. The burning rain disintegrated any sense of moral accountability. Middleton and Walsh put it this way:

> Within the context of postmodernity . . . this retreat from moral accountability and retirement to self-indulgence is perfectly understandable. Postmodernity is, after all, a "mall culture." And, like carnivals, shopping malls can be exhausting. Being bombarded with a cacophony of voices, each calling us to enter into their world, and constantly being required to make world and identity-constructing choices before the postmodern smorgasbord results in a widespread feeling of consumer exhaustion.[35]

Self-indulgence is what "The Playboy Mansion" appears to portray. Stokes interprets this song as "a powerful image of the spiritual collapse of a world where everybody wants more, and your worth is ultimately measured according to your ability to spend . . . on yourself."[36] If the superficial subjects of this song are what our culture claims as significant, then we have adopted a Zooropian worldview, and little hope is left. *If beauty is truth / And surgery the fountain of youth / What am I to do.*[37]

There is more to this song than the borrowing of the advertising world's slogans and pop culture's clichés. As nonchalant as "The Playboy Mansion" sounds, and as shallow as it pretends to be, the wandering soul is still looking to fill that God-shaped hole. The gates of the Playboy Mansion and the casino-like setting of the song are plastic parallels of the Kingdom of God. Beyond the cultural reference points,

> the song is infused with a real sense of spiritual yearning, as if at some deep level the covetous protagonist knows that it's all fake, that far from being even better than the real thing, his desires are but a pale shadow of the heart's need for a more fulfilling kind of truth. Or perhaps that's just Bono's real voice coming through when he confesses *'And though I can't say why / I've got to believe.'*[38]

---

[35] Middleton & Walsh, *Truth is Stranger Than it Used to Be*, 60.
[36] Stokes, *Into the Heart*, 135.
[37] "The Playboy Mansion," from the album *Pop*. © 1997 Polygram International Music BV.
[38] Stokes, *Into the Heart*, 135.

Even through their satirical masks, U2's honesty breaks out. The protagonist believes in more than his lucky day, when *the colours come flashing / and the lights go on*. He does not know why, but he has to believe in something greater. Talking about the juxtaposition of Bono's stage alter-egos while performing earnest songs (e.g., "Pride" with Martin Luther King on video screens behind the band) the Edge reflects, "Amid the uncertainty there are certain ideas that are so powerful and so right that you can hold onto them no matter how screwed up everything else is."[39]

In the middle of a "screwed up" Zooropian culture, the powerful eschatological themes of *The Joshua Tree* resurface. The exhausted Wanderer is spiritually dislocated. He needs an anchor. He needs something real in which to place whatever hope he has left. Perhaps another double entendre can be seen in *the colours come flashing / and the lights go on*. Could this be a description of one of John's visions?

> And He who was sitting was like a jasper stone and a sardius in appearance; and there was a rainbow around the throne, like an emerald in appearance. And from the throne proceed flashes of lightning and sounds of and peals of thunder. (Revelation 4:3, 5a)

The time of sorrow, pain, and shame will not be removed by accumulating more material wealth. The Wanderer has realized that there is more. If love were to "come on down," then would there be no time of sorrow, pain, and shame.

> And I heard a loud voice from the throne, saying,
> "See, the home of God is among mortals,
> He will dwell among them as their God;
> they will be his peoples,
> and God himself will be with them;
> he will wipe every tear from their eyes.
> Death will be no more;
> mourning and crying and pain will be no more,
> for the first things have passed away."

---

[39] DeCurtis, "*Zooropa* Album Review: *Zooropa* Mon Amour," 215.

And the one who was seated on the throne said,
"See, I am making all things new." (Revelation 21:3-5a)

The protagonist fears that he might not make it to Christ's restoration (*don't know if I can hold on / don't know if I'm that strong / don't know if I can wait that long*). "Those who conquer will inherit these things, and I will be their God and they will be my children."[40] Yahweh offers infinitely more than all of Zooropa's casinos and brothels put together. He offers covenant. He offers himself.

Pop concludes with the Wanderer's lament. The party has come to a grinding halt. It is the next morning. The Wanderer is hung over and all alone. Where is Jesus? Did he take the Wanderer's advice and not wait up for him? Is he still sleeping? Is he not strong enough to overpower the Antichrist and his city of Babylon? Will this time of shalom ever come or was it just a made up story to string us along. The Wanderer joins in with the sons of Korah and sings this closing lament. *Jesus, Jesus help me / I'm alone in this world / . . . / tell me, tell me the story / the one about eternity / and the way it's all gonna be.*[41]

"*Pop* begins on a high. 'Discothèque' is bright, contemporary, and in your face. At least on the surface, it is a hedonistic celebration of the ephemeral . . . But from that acknowledgement of worldly addictions on, the record journeys down—from dance to despair."[42] Acknowledging the need for a grand story (*tell me, tell me the story / the one about eternity / and the way it's all gonna be*), "Wake Up Dead Man" is analogous to Psalm 44. This psalm is a lament, and, therefore, also a psalm of disorientation. The laments are

> speeches of surprised dismay and disappointment for the speaker never expected this to happen to him or her. They are fresh utterances, sharp ejaculations . . . They are the shrill speeches of those who suddenly discover that they are trapped and the water is rising and the sun may not come up tomorrow in all its benevolence. And we are betrayed.[43]

---

[40] Revelation 21:7.
[41] "Wake Up Dead Man," from the album *Pop*. © 1997 Polygram International Music BV.
[42] Stokes, *Into the Heart*, 138.
[43] Brueggemann, *The Psalms and the Life of Faith*, 19.

"People want to believe but they're angry," rants Bono. "If God is not dead, there's some questions we want to ask him."[44]

"Wake Up Dead Man" reveals the loneliness in a broken, hurting world. It prays to Jesus to remember the covenant by recounting the foundational narrative.[45] The song is played over another audio record that is reminiscent of mournful wailing. This distorted effect only amplifies the desperation of the lament. The singer asks Jesus to listen over this noise to hear the pain of those suffering in this broken world. The composers of Psalm 44 shared the same questions. In the face of injustice they cried out,

> Rouse yourself! Why do you sleep, O Lord?
>> Awake, do not cast us off forever!
> Why do you hide your face?
>> Why do you forget our affliction and oppression?
> For we sink down to the dust;
>> our bodies cling to the ground.
> Rise up, come to our help.
>> Redeem us for the sake of your steadfast love. (Psalm 44:23-26)

Both Psalm 44 and "Wake Up Dead Man" end in a perplexed state of disorientation. Faith and hope hang on long enough to pray to Yahweh. Yet both songs end with his silence.

It appears that at this point, U2 is beginning to leave irony behind. Does this album mark the end of U2's role as cultural barometer? I would argue that it does. In the wake of the two following albums, U2 move beyond taking the pulse of the culture, and begin to offer a remedy. Their following albums are unlike any of their past endeavors. Instead of simply commenting, the next album actually breaks new ground by also providing a positive, cultural/spiritual model for living. With Brueggemann as our guide, *All That You Can't Leave Behind* and *How to Dismantle an Atomic Bomb* could easily be classified as new orientation. God appears to be silent, but only for a time. The season of joy is about to begin.

---

[44] Stokes, *Into the Heart*, 139.
[45] Psalm 44:1-8 recounts Israel's foundational narrative.

5
Recapturing Imagination

"God is in the room . . . It feels like there's a blessing on the band right now. And I don't know what it is, but it feels like God walking through the room, and it feels like a blessing, and in the end, music is a kind of sacrament; it's not just about airplay or chart positions."
—Bono[1]

"Call to Me, and I will answer you,
and I will tell you great and mighty things, which you do not know."[2]

In the tradition of Ezra and Haggai, *All That You Can't Leave Behind* is about the journey home. For the Israelites, it was an exodus from Babylon and a return to Zion. For us, it is a departure from the mind-numbing bogs of Zooropa and a reoriented journey toward the Kingdom of God. Our Zooropa is Christian's Vanity Fair.[3] Though the quagmire of *Pop* was a deeper excursion into U2's constructed disorientation, it left lyrical clues

---

[1] Heath, "U2 Tour: From the Heart," *Rolling Stone*, 10 May 2001.
[2] Jeremiah 33:3 (The reference "J33-3" is superimposed in the background of U2's album cover *All That You Can't Leave Behind*.)
[3] Thanks to John Bunyan's *Pilgrim's Progress* for its marvelous metaphors illustrating Christian's journey to the Celestial City.

that pointed in the direction of the band's next endeavour. In "Gone" we find the title and theme of U2's subsequent album: *You change a name but that's okay . . . it's necessary/ and what you leave behind you don't miss anyway.*[4]

ATYCLB is the realization that to move beyond Zooropa one has to leave behind all the things acquired through the deception of greed, envy, and self-aggrandizement.[5] In a movement from lament to praise, *ATYCLB* has U2 shedding its satirical skin, leaving the band open and vulnerable. Following Wim Wenders advice U2 has abandoned irony. Plain speaking is necessary now. Communication should be direct, and anything that might create confusion should be eschewed.[6]

A Fresh Start in Zooropa

In *ATYCLB*, U2 abandons the grief-filled language of hopelessness and adopts the language of amazement. This language of amazement is against the despair of Zooropa, just as the language of grief was against Zooropa's numbness.[7] The contrast between "Wake Up Dead Man" (*Pop*'s closing song) and "Beautiful Day" (*ATYCLB*'s opening number) is a perfect example of Brueggemann's languages of despair and amazement. The title alone, "Beautiful Day," speaks of hope. Daniel Lanois likens the song to a hymn. He believes the song has hymnic qualities "in its backbone."[8]

Note well, however, the landscape of Zooropa still provides the context for this song. The ground is still baked and the city still congested as we find ourselves stuck in the gridlock, *ready to let go of the steering wheel.*[9] The absence of a destination, the mud, and the self-constructed maze of imagination of the second verse are all metaphors transposed from "Zooropa." The uncertainty of the postmodern condition has not been a "guiding light." Ambiguous self-constructed realities have only led to aimless wandering in the ridiculous mazes of stifled imaginations.

---

[4] "Gone," from the album *Pop*. © 1997 Polygram International Music BV.

[5] Jesus said, "Beware, and be on your guard against every form of greed; for not even when one has abundance does his life consist of his possessions" (Luke 12:15).

[6] Stockman citing Wim Wenders, *Walk On*, 165.

[7] Brueggemann, *The Prophetic Imagination*, 67–68.

[8] Stokes, *Into the Heart*, 147.

[9] "Zoo Station," from the album *Achtung Baby*. © 1991 Island Records.

Uncertainty still abounds in the shadow of Zooropa. Nonetheless, sunshine breaks its way through the atomic sky. *The heart is a bloom, shoots up through the stony ground / But there's no room, no space to rent in this town / You're out of luck and the reason that you had to care / The traffic is stuck and you're not moving anywhere.*[10]

From the mournful wailing of "Wake up Dead Man" to the joyful sound of "Beautiful Day," *ATYCLB* challenges the dominant worldview of Zooropa.[11] The album can be compared to John's Revelation, which Bauckham and Hart describe as an alternative picture full of the "potentialities and possibilities inherent in God's future."[12] Like Revelation, *ATYCLB* is "an imaginative vision in which the dominant way of seeing things (both present and future) is fundamentally challenged."[13] The lament of "Wake up Dead Man" receives an unexpected response through "Beautiful Day."

Through the hardened, stony ground, a bloom shoots up. After the flood all the colours come out. "Beautiful Day" is the psalmist's song of reorientation. God's response to the "Where are you?" questions in "Wake up Dead Man" is found in his covenantal love. This is evidenced in the Incarnation. Where is Jesus? He is here with us. He is the shoot that springs from the stem of Jesse.[14] He is the tender shoot, and he is like a root growing out of parched ground.[15] It is a beautiful day for the psalmist because he realizes that God Incarnate is the bloom that has quietly sprung up into the land of Zooropa, Babylon, Rome, Bethlehem. Yes, even though Zooropa is the setting for this song, the singer can shout subversively "It's

---

[10] "Beautiful Day," from the album *All That You Can't Leave Behind.* © 2000 Universal International Music BV.

[11] Chris Heath, "U2: Band of the Year." Bono acknowledges the contrast between the "trilogy" and *ATYCLB*. "He tries to explain how he'd like their new record to be. 'Joy!' he hollers. 'Happiness means nothing—happiness means getting rid of a headache. Joy is another thing altogether' . . . He waves his hand, explaining how in the Nineties, U2 wandered away from joy—'We got darker and darker, but the lights were all the brighter at our concerts.'"

[12] Bauckham & Hart, *Hope Against Hope*, 197.

[13] Ibid.

[14] Isaiah 11:1.

[15] Isaiah 53:2.

a beautiful day!" because of his God-initiated covenant.[16] In the face of
the Babylonian Empire, Isaiah proclaimed a similar song of hope.

> Have you not known? Have you not heard?
> The LORD is the Everlasting God,
> the Creator of the ends of the earth.
> He does not faint or grow weary;
> his understanding is unsearchable.
> He gives power to the faint,
> and strengthens the powerless.
> Even youths will faint and be weary,
> and the young will fall exhausted;
> but those who wait for the LORD
> shall renew their strength,
> they shall mount up with wings like eagles,
> they shall run and not be weary,
> they shall walk and not faint. (Isaiah 40:28-31)

Just as the singer in "Wake up Dead Man" asks Jesus to listen over the
noise to hear the pain of those suffering in this broken world, the voice in
"Beautiful Day" prays that Yahweh might remember his covenant with
humanity and creation, made with Noah after the flood: *See the Bedouin
fires at night / See the oil fields at first light / See the bird with a leaf in her
mouth / After the flood all the colours came out.* Who else could have such a
vantage point of all of creation besides God?[17] It is Yahweh who is reminded
of the dove with the freshly picked olive leaf in her beak. He is reminded
of the rainbow of colours he himself placed in the sky as a sign of covenant
between him and creation.

---

[16] Bud Osborn, "Amazingly Alive," from *Hundred Block Rock* (Vancouver: Arsenal Pulp
Press, 1999) 7–11. In the face of a North American culture, Osborn offers a more abrasive,
yet similar poem of subversion: *shout here we are/ amazingly alive/ against long odds/ left
for dead/ shoutin this death culture/ dancin this death culture/ out of our heads.*
[17] "Who has measured the waters in the hollow of His hand, and marked off the heavens
by the span, and calculated the dust of the earth by the measure, and weighed the
mountains in a balance, and the hills in a pair of scales?" (Isaiah 40:12). "The LORD is
in His holy temple; the LORD's throne is in heaven" (Psalm 11:4a).

The singer continues with a double plea for intimacy (with Yahweh) and translocation *(Touch me, take me to that other place)*. That other place is the Kingdom of God, *where the streets have no name.* Very appropriately, U2 reverts to eschatological language. Its usage is timely.

> Eschatology is above all a source of hope and liberation, and is addressed, therefore, to those who, in one way or another, find themselves in the grip of hopelessness, slavery or oppression . . . It is no accident, therefore, that much of the explicitly eschatological literature in the Bible was written during periods of exile and persecution. It is directly political in nature, designed to shape the actions of the oppressed by capturing their imaginations and offering a transforming vision of God's promised future.[18]

At that promised future, that final destination, whatever you do not have with you, you no longer need. Here the listener finds one of the key themes on *ATYCLB*. It is the idea of letting go of material wealth, ethereal knowledge, and social status. It is allowing God to shatter the shackles of Scientism, Technicism, and Economism and believing that he will *lift me out of these blues* and *tell me something true.*[19] Yahweh restores feeling to a deadened body and a numb mind. He gives the Wanderer a purpose, a destination, a new name. No longer Wanderer, the new name given is Sojourner. The destination is Home. The journey is long and the secret is to travel light.

Lightening the Load

Aung San Suu Kyi is a Burmese woman who was living under virtual house arrest. Leaving her husband, her son, and a comfortable position at Oxford University, Aung San Suu Kyi returned to Burma and became the leader of the National League for Democracy that mounted the campaign against Burma's corrupt military junta. In 1989 she was placed under

---

[18] Bauckham & Hart, *Hope Against Hope,* 193.
[19] "Elevation," from the album *All That You Can't Leave Behind.* © 2000 Universal International Music BV.

house arrest. In 1991, while still under house arrest, this hero was awarded the Nobel Peace Prize. Up until 1995, Aung San Suu Kyi was unable to receive visitors or communicate freely.[20]

"Walk On" was inspired by and is dedicated to Aung San Suu Kyi. Reflecting on her decision, Bono called it "one of the great acts of courage of the twentieth century . . . and it continues into the twenty-first."[21] U2's "Walk On" video concludes with Aung San Suu Kyi (via satellite link) saying, "This is not yet the end. There's a long way to go and the way might be very, very hard. So, please stand by."[22] *Walk on, walk on / What you got they can't steal it / No they can't even feel it / . . . / What you've got they can't deny it / Can't sell it, can't buy it.*[23]

Stokes observes that, "Aung San Suu Kyi's journey becomes a point of departure in itself, a springboard towards the realisation that in the end we're all going to have to leave baggage that we create or accumulate behind, as we undertake the final journey to whatever home awaits us in the beyond."[24] *Leave it behind,* and the "Beautiful Day" lyric, *What you don't have you don't need it now,* ring true with Christ's parable of the selfish farmer who built bigger barns to hoard his crops. Setting the tone for the story, Jesus warned, "Take care! Be on your guard against all kinds of greed; for one's life does not consist in the abundance of possessions" (Luke 12:15).

Originally meant to be a love song between Aung San Suu Kyi and her family, "Walk On" has taken on a larger meaning. *You're packing a suitcase for a place none of us has been* not only speaks of the song's heroine leaving for Burma, but also of those who have sojourned into the uncharted regions of that "better country."[25] Aside from leaving family behind to pursue a greater cause, this song ultimately speaks of death.

---

[20] Stokes, *Into the Heart*, 151.

[21] Ibid.

[22] Aung San Suu Kyi, from U2's *Walk On* DVD single. © 2001 Universal International Music BV.

[23] "Walk On," from the album *All That You Can't Leave Behind*. © 2000 Universal International Music BV.

[24] Stokes, *Into the Heart*, 152.

[25] See Hebrews 11:13-16.

"Just the essential things," says Bono. "The stuff you can take with you: friendship, laughter. Wisdom, if you've found any." If there is one thing that suffuses the record, it is a sense of mortality, of how and what you treasure in a world where death awaits . . . "You know, the record we were trying to make was quite a bit more joyful and about a certain kind of love of life and vitality," says the Edge. "And that's in there, but there's also this other side, which sort of crept into the record almost without me noticing. And if the record was about breaking things back down to essentials, I suppose in the end mortality is the ultimate inescapable fact of life."[26]

After the death of his father in August 2001, "Walk On" took on a deeper personal dimension for Bono. "Clearly, only those who anguish will sing new songs. Without anguish the new song is likely to be strident and just more royal fakery."[27] Death is the door through which the Sojourner must pass in order to reach her destination. As final as death wants to be, there is more. "Home" is beyond death. This revolutionary thought can only be expressed because of Jesus Christ's own death and resurrection. This way of thinking is subversive and "counter Empire." If Scientism, Technicism, and Economism are demi-gods of the Empire, then Sin, Death, and Fear are the Empire's high gods. As Bauckham and Hart explain,

Death will get us in the end . . . All that exists is characterized by transience and the movement toward its own eventual demise. Nothing finally endures. Thus the resurrection of Jesus from death is, more than any other single event, or combination of events in his life, a breach of the 'orderliness' of this world which scandalizes and turns our view of the whole of reality upside down. If we admit its reality then it leaves nothing the same. Its reality is one which disrupts the pattern of sin and death.[28]

In the triumphant spirit of the resurrection, "Walk On" proclaims the new song of hope. It disrupts the distracting demi-gods of Zooropa, reminding us that there is more to this life than daily consumption. The

---

[26] Heath, "U2: Band of the Year."
[27] Brueggemann, *The Prophetic Imagination*, 79.
[28] Bauckham & Hart, *Hope Against Hope*, 103.

song is a declaration that the stranglehold of Sin and Death has been countered and defeated. And yet, despite its hope-filled resonances, "Walk On" is full of heartache and yearning.

The longing is for God's promised future, our true home. *Home . . . hard to know what it is if you've never had one / Home . . . I can't say where it is but I know I'm going home / That's where the hurt is.* "Walk On" admits, with Aung San Suu Kyi, that "this is not yet the end; there's a long way to go, and the way might be very, very hard." *That's where the hurt is* could be better defined as "the ache that stems from the longing for God's Kingdom." Used intratexually, "In a Little While" echoes this longing and anticipates an end to the pain (*In a little while/ This hurt will hurt no more/ I'll be home, love.*)[29]

Until that destination is reached, we are encouraged to walk on. Do not wander. Walk ahead with purpose. Leave behind any cumbersome baggage that may slow us down.[30] *And if the darkness is to keep us apart / And if the daylight feels like it's a long way off / And if your glass heart should crack / And for a second you turn back / Oh no, be strong.* What we have cannot be stolen. It is sealed with God. This "prize" cannot be touched, for the idols of the empire cannot feel, taste, see, or hear.[31] The few things that accompany the Sojourner on the long way home are her very sources of strength: a relationship with the living God, a caravan of community, and a true sense of life's fleetingness. From wandering the endless wilderness of Zooropa to journeying toward God's Country, our protagonist has come a long way. She has learned much since embarking on the narrow road. The following can be read as a poem of accumulated wisdom meant to encourage her fellow travelers as they together make their way homeward.

Eternally Yahweh's

Released as a B-side on the *Beautiful Day* single, "Always" is an appropriate coda to this musical journey.[32] When all is said and done, this song identifies

---

[29] "In a Little While," from the album *All That You Can't Leave Behind.* © 2000 Universal International Music BV.

[30] Hebrews 12:1.

[31] Psalm 115:1-8.

[32] "Always," from the single *Beautiful Day.* © 2000 Universal International Music BV.

the essential "carry-ons" required for the journey to God's Country. It is a song of letting go, not fretting about things lost. This is a song written at the borderland between Zooropa and That Other Place. Brueggemann writes:

> Israel's prayer characteristically happens at the limits. Doxology occurs at the limit of *glad self-abandonment*, when God is all in all. Lament occurs at the limit of *anguished self-insistence*, when God must yield in costly ways and care in powerful ways for the speaker in need. Both aspects of prayer in gratitude and amazement, in anguish and insistence, are "pray-backs" to the creed, celebrations of God's [loving kindness] so visible or insistence on God's [loving kindness] so absent.[33]

At the limits, "Always" finds itself in the category of doxology and glad self-abandonment. The song begins with a relentless biblical honesty (*Here today, gone tomorrow/ Crack the bone, get to the marrow*).[34] The song gets to the important details of the journey. Yes, the journey may seem long, but in light of the destination, it is rather brief. Therefore, put positively, the essentials for the journey are an awareness of one's own brevity, glad self-abandonment (*Be the arrow and the target/ Put your head over the parapet*), inner beauty, community (*This is the moment that we share*), and humility (*Get down off your holy cloud/ God will not deal with the proud*).[35] These are the necessities that the Sojourner will keep. Anything else that has been lost is not needed, not worth losing a moment's sleep over.

The phrase "dream out loud" was previously encountered in "Zooropa" (*She's gonna dream up/ The world she wants to live in/ She's gonna dream out loud*). Dreaming out loud in Zooropa is constructing one's own reality, whereas dreaming out loud on the Way consists of prayer to Yahweh (*Turning [each song] slowly into a prayer*). What better way to end that prayer than with a fastened *amen* in the form of *Eternally yours, Now and forever/ for always*. Dreaming out loud gives public voice to an alternative

---

[33] Brueggemann, *The Psalms and the Life of Faith*, 57.

[34] Cf. Isaiah 40:6-8, 1 Peter 1:24, and James 4:14 on humanity's transience.

[35] Cf. Psalm 138:6, Proverbs 3:34, James 4:6, and 1 Peter 5:6 on God's preference of the humble over the proud.

imagination, which this book suggests that U2 continues to fulfill throughout their own musical journey. In the Sojourner's prayer, the journey is far from over. In fact, U2's subsequent album, *How to Dismantle an Atomic Bomb,* provides the Sojourner with prayers for the narrow road. They help refine what can and cannot be taken along on this trip.

6

Prayers for the Journey Home

"If you want to kiss the sky, better learn how to kneel"[1]

"So tired of all this travelling,
so many miles away from home,
I keep moving to be stable."[2]

"Oh don't sorrow, no don't weep
for tonight, at last
I am coming home
I am coming home"[3]

Raw, personal, uncomfortably intimate. Not the typical adjectives used to describe a rock and roll album. Yet this is precisely the way *How to Dismantle an Atomic Bomb (HTDAAB)* comes across. It sounds as if U2

---

[1] "Mysterious Ways," from the album *Achtung Baby.* © 1991 Island Records Ltd.
[2] Peter Gabriel, "Sky Blue," from the album *Up.* © 2002 Geffen Records.
[3] "A Sort of Homecoming," from the album *The Unforgettable Fire.* © 1984 Island Records Ltd.

are wearing their hearts on their sleeves again. When listening to "Sometimes You Can't Make it On Your Own," a song written for and performed at the funeral of Bono's father, Bob Hewson, one can't help but feel like the singer's life is being poured out for all to see. We're offered uncomfortable, almost awkward glimpses into the singer's soul. How does a listener respond to the lyric sung to Bono's father, *I don't need to hear you say / That if we weren't so alike / You'd like me a whole lot more?* It was very bold of the band to incorporate such a transparent song within the album. Its riveting honesty hits the listener on several levels and causes him to take stock of the relationships life has to offer. But this is not the only song that exposes us to a vulnerable side of U2. The album is also peppered with petitions and prayers to the Most High God. From the dizzying "Vertigo" *(Your love is teaching me how, how to kneel),* to the anchored "Yahweh" *(Take this heart / And make it break), HTDAAB* offers the listener prayers she can adopt as her own *(God I need your help tonight[4], You can make me perfect again / All because of you . . . I am[5], and I kneel 'cos I want you some more / I want the lot of what you got/ And I want nothing that you're not).*[6]

Referring to *HTDAAB,* the Edge comments, "Even if it's not necessarily overtly about what's happening now, I think in a major way there is an undercurrent that pervades the whole album."[7] Indeed, as discussed of previous albums concerning the first and last songs (*Zooropa's* "Zooropa" and "The Wanderer," *Pop's* "Discothèque" and "Wake Up Dead Man," *ATYCLB's* "Beautiful Day" and "Grace"), "Vertigo" and "Yahweh" become the ideal bookends of *HTDAAB.* They highlight the main theme and thrust of the album. The following will examine that underlying theme woven throughout this album. As mentioned in the last chapter, on this path of reorientation, the Sojourner leaves behind cumbersome baggage. The things that accompany her along the way are a relationship with the living God, a caravan of community, and a true sense of life's fleetingness.

---

[4] "Miracle Drug," from the album *How to Dismantle an Atomic Bomb.* © 2004 Universal International Music BV.
[5] "All Because of You," from the album *How to Dismantle an Atomic Bomb.* © 2004 Universal International Music BV.
[6] "Original of the Species," from the album *How to Dismantle an Atomic Bomb.* © 2004 Universal International Music BV.
[7] Andrew Mueller, ed. *U2 Vertigo 2005 Tour Programme.* 2005.

HTDAAB throws in an extra essential for the journey; a necessary attitude for the road. Considering this self-indulgent age of individualism and egoism, of personal rights and freedoms, this item may seem somewhat awkward. It is brokenness. It is humility. And it is required to offer perspective and feeling for the Sojourner.

Teach Me How to Kneel

If Bill Flanagan was correct in saying that the songs of *Achtung Baby* could be interpreted as being about a woman or God, then "Mysterious Ways" takes on a higher meaning. The lyrics from this song, *If you want to kiss the sky, better learn how to kneel/ On your knees boy,* can be tied together with those from "Always"—*get down off your holy cloud/ God will not deal with the proud.* These lyrics are borrowed from Proverbs 3:34, "Toward the scorners he is scornful, but to the humble he shows favor," and 1 Peter 5:5, "God opposes the proud but gives grace to the humble." Though the next song may read and sound like a return to disorientation, do not be deceived. Despite its title and roller coaster vibe, "Vertigo" sheds light on life beyond disorientation. *I'm at a place called Vertigo (¿Dondé estas?) / It's everything I wish I didn't know / Except you give me something I can feel, feel.*[8]

Darkness, jungles, strobe lights, loud beats, swinging to the music, where are we? Have we returned to the discothèque? Are we retreating into the bowels of Zooropa? This does not feel right. Where on earth is Vertigo? The construct of what constitutes a worldview may shed some light and aid us in placing our traveler. As discussed in chapter 3, the answers to the four basic questions *(Who am I? Where am I? What's wrong? What's the remedy?),* help establish one's reason for being. Who am I? I am a Sojourner. No longer am I a Wanderer without goal or purpose. I now have a driving force within me. I now have a destination. Where am I? I'm at a place called Vertigo. Bono says of Vertigo,

---

[8] "Vertigo," from the album *How to Dismantle an Atomic Bomb.* © 2004 Universal International Music BV.

In my head I created a club called Vertigo, with all these people in it and the music is not the music you want to hear, and the people are not the people you want to be with, and then you see somebody and she's got a cross around her neck, and you focus on it, because you can't focus on anything else. You find a little tiny fragment of salvation there.[9]

Vertigo is a place in a desert, a wilderness.[10] It is a place of trial and testing along the Sojourner's way. With its bridge—*All of this, all of this can be yours/ Just give me what I want and no-one gets hurt*—the song evokes memories of Christ's wilderness trials.[11] Introducing the devil's tempting voice is reminiscent of Bono's Macphisto days of Zooropa. The bridge may not precisely pinpoint our location, but it does drive home the reason for our being in Vertigo. What's wrong? If we follow this train of thought, then the Vertigo Wilderness becomes a place of testing. And after forty days and nights without food or water, the Sojourner is feeling famished and thirsty, with many more obstacles yet to overcome. The full effects of Vertigo are taking their toll, and the destination has not yet been reached. What's the remedy? Amidst the confusion of Club Vertigo, a glimmer of hope is found. This cross, a symbol of salvation, reflects the strobes and mirror ball lights as it dangles around someone's neck. It is a reminder that there is hope beyond this shell of a club. It is not the destination, only a stopover along the way.

How do we know that the Sojourner hasn't relapsed to his aimless wandering days? Doubt permeates the song *(And though your soul/ It can't be bought/ Your mind can wander).* Yet due to its declarative nature, "Vertigo" is a song of reorientation.[12] Despite the confusion, the darkness, the murmuring voices, and the jungle in the head, the singer declares that he can feel. Were he back in Zooropa, there would be only numbness. The calloused, scarred heart of Zooropa's Wanderer cannot feel. He can only consume, saying, "Gimme some more. Too much is not enough to fill this GOD-shaped hole." Our Sojourner, however, declares to God, "You give me something! Something I can feel! Feel!" With the lights

---

[9] Andrew Mueller, ed. *U2 Vertigo 2005 Tour Programme.* 2005.
[10] U2's primary "Vertigo" video was shot in the desert.
[11] Cf. Matthew 4:1-11, Mark 1:12-13, and Luke 4:1-13.
[12] Brueggemann, *The Psalms & the Life of Faith*, 24.

down, in the dark, there is something to hold onto. A way out can be found with this gift of "something."

This gift is declared at the song's conclusion. The way through Vertigo is love. Not just anyone's love, but Yahweh's covenant love. This is the sort of love that gives tireless chase to its prey. God desires to give his love to all. *You can run from love / And if it's really love it will find you / Catch you by the heel / But you can't be numb for love / The only pain is to feel nothing at all.*[13]

God gives his love freely to all, and because of its very nature it teaches us how to feel, causing us to kneel. The love of God is expressed most clearly through his Son, Jesus Christ, who offered his life for humanity and all of creation.[14] When confronted with such amazingly surprising love, what other response can there be, except to fall down and kneel? The Million Dollar Hotel Band's "Falling At Your Feet" revolves around this very idea.[15] *Every eye closed by a bruise / Every player who just can't lose / Every pop star hurling abuse / Every drunk back on the booze / All falling at your feet / I'm falling at your feet.*[16]

We are told in both the Old and New Testaments of the Bible that a day will come when all of creation, all of humanity, will collapse in awe before God.[17] In its conclusion, "Falling At Your Feet" offers listeners a key to accepting God's gift of love. *How to navigate [through Vertigo]? / How might I be still [and know peace]? / Teach me to surrender. / Not my will, thy will.*[18] To get through the trial, one must learn to let go, to kneel. From the gift of God's love springs the gift of humility and brokenness. It is only in this state of brokenness that one can begin to adopt and apply

---

[13] "A Man and a Woman," from the album *How to Dismantle an Atomic Bomb*. © 2004 Universal International Music BV.

[14] "Just as the Son of Man came not to be served but to serve, and to give his life a ransom for many," Matthew 20:28.

[15] The MDH Band consists of Bono, Daniel Lanois, Jon Hassel, Brian Eno, Greg Cohen, Brian Blade, Adam Dorn, and Bill Frisell. Additional musicians include Brad Mehldau and Chris Spedding.

[16] "Falling At Your Feet," from the soundtrack *The Million Dollar Hotel*. © 2000 Universal Island Records Ltd. Recommended listening: Daniel Lanois' version of "Falling At Your Feet," from the album *Shine*. © 2003 Anti, Inc.

[17] Cf. Isaiah 45:23, Romans 14:11.

[18] Borrowed from Christ's prayer in the Garden of Gethsemane. Cf. Matthew 26:36-46, Mark 14:32-42, Luke 22:39-46.

Christ's highest commands, "Love the Lord your God with all your passion and prayer and intelligence. This is the most important, the first on any list. But there is a second to set alongside it: Love others as well as you love yourself."[19] The confession and prayer of "Teach me how to kneel" is also offered up in the song "Love and Peace or Else" *(I don't know if I can make it, I'm not easy on my knees)*. In this song, however, confessing her inflexibility *(I'm not easy on my knees)*, the Sojourner extends her prayer.

Take this Heart and Make it Break

With its contradictory title, and the disconnect between its lyrics and score, "Love and Peace or Else" fulfills its expectations on several levels. Its abrasive sound is the "or else" to its rather submissive lyric of *love and peace*. Referencing the conflict in the Middle East, it also implies that there won't be any "love and peace" unless the "or else" is buried. No resolution will be arrived at without a surrendering on both sides. The song's beginning could be referencing two peoples at war, a lover, or Jesus himself. It's only by risking everything and corporately laying love on the track that the monster, be it war, conflict, or the devil, will be overcome. *Lay your love on the track / We're gonna break the monster's back.*[20]

As we have seen and heard so far, U2's songs are multi-layered and can be interpreted on an intratextual level. Whereas "Love and Peace or Else" could be defined as a political song, pleading for peace in the Middle East, it can also be understood on a much deeper, more personal level. And in the same vein as "Walk On," it calls the Sojourner to leave everything behind *(lay down your treasure / lay it down now brother)*, echoing Christ's words, "For what will a man be profited, if he gains the whole world, and forfeits his soul? Or what will a man give in exchange for his soul?"[21] As if whispering to a newborn baby, the song offers the prayer: *As you enter this life / I pray you depart / With a wrinkled face / And a brand*

---

[19] Matthew 22:37-39 (The Message).
[20] "Love and Peace or Else," from the album *How to Dismantle an Atomic Bomb.* © 2004 Universal International Music BV.
[21] Matthew 16:26 (NASB).

new heart. It is reminiscent of words written by the Old Testament prophet Ezekiel:

> I will give them an undivided heart
> > and put a new spirit in them;
> I will remove from them their heart of stone
> > and give them a heart of flesh.[22]

Later on in Ezekiel, God reiterates, saying, "Rid yourselves of all the offences you have committed, and get a new heart and a new spirit."[23] On the one hand we read of God promising to do the work of transforming the inner person, and on the other of God telling us to do it ourselves. How is this possible? Is this a divine cop-out? Is God saying he isn't capable of doing what he promised? I would argue not.

Referring back to "Drowning Man," God is more than willing to rescue the drowning man caught up in the winds and waves. Yet that willingness needs to be mutual. God says, "Take my hand." He has his hand extended, ready to aid. All that needs to be done is to grab hold. The human race was not created as a collective of automatons. God will not impose himself on humanity. Rather, he wishes to partner with us, to come alongside of us and guide us on our journey toward him. This is reflected in the passages from Ezekiel. Yes, God will transform our hearts. He will shatter the stone hard heart of war, malice, selfishness, pride, hatred, and bitterness, and replace it with a brand new heart of peace, kindness, generosity, humility, love, and sweetness. All that is required is surrender. Once the Sojourner is penitent of his offences, his wrongdoings, and offers his heart, his entire being to God, the breaking and renewal can begin. The much-needed release, release, release can finally occur. For the broken heart is what God truly loves. It is his tilling ground.

> The sacrifice acceptable to God is a broken spirit;
> a broken and contrite heart, O God, you will not despise.[24]

---

[22] Ezekiel 11:19.
[23] Ezekiel 18:31.
[24] Psalm 51:17.

With all this talk of the heart, what is it exactly? What constitutes the heart? Well, the closing song of *HTDAAB* offers an excellent definition of the heart. If it is possible, the Sojourner's prayer becomes even more intimate on "Yahweh." Calling "Yahweh" a prayer, the Edge admits, "I really can't explain it beyond that, it's one of those songs that had to be written, and again we just got out of the way."[25] Described as a "modern hymn with a broadband connection to God," "Yahweh" anchors the album by driving home its main theme of surrender.[26] *Take this soul / Stranded in some skin and bones / Take this soul / And make it sing.*[27]

"Yahweh" is a parallel to *Pop*'s "Do You Feel Loved."[28] Both songs offer the themes of intimacy and surrender. "Do You Feel Loved" explores the intimacy and bond between a man and a woman, whereas "Yahweh" reveals the intimacy between a man and God. They exhibit numerous intratextual comparisons. Instead of the questioning lyric, *Do you feel loved?*, "Yahweh" concludes with the prayer *Take this heart / And make it break*. In other words, "I have felt your love, Yahweh. You give me something I can feel. Your love is teaching me how to kneel, to surrender, how to give up my rights for the other. Take what no man can own. Take my heart and break it."

Let's return to our unanswered question of what constitutes the heart. Besides the obvious answer of being a critical organ necessary for life, depending on how far back one goes, the heart can be defined in a variety ways. New Testament writers thought the heart to be the centre of a person's spiritual and emotional identity. The words *heart* and *mind* are often found together denoting the emotional and psychological elements of a person's make-up. The ancient poet Homer considered the heart to be the center of a person's will, enabling the power of choice. Jewish men and women who penned the Old Testament had a more unified understanding of the heart. The heart, from a Hebrew perspective, defined the person in her totality. It is a term that encompasses every aspect of the human being.[29]

---

[25] Andrew Mueller, ed. *U2 Vertigo 2005 Tour Programme.* 2005.

[26] Adrian Deevoy, "U2 Walk on Water," *Blender*, November 2004, 122.

[27] "Yahweh," from the album *How to Dismantle an Atomic Bomb.* © 2004 Universal International Music BV.

[28] "Do You Feel Loved," from the album *Pop.* © 1997 Polygram International Music BV.

[29] Colin Brown, ed., *The New International Dictionary of New Testament Theology*, vol. 2, (Grand Rapids: Zondervan, 1976), 180–84.

It is with this Hebrew understanding, I believe, that "Yahweh" is sung. Notice everything that the singer offers to Yahweh? From clothing, to hands and feet that perform deeds, to mouths that verbalize ideas and intent, to the very soul. The heart that the singer surrenders is his entire being. He has been offering it to be transformed throughout the song.

Despite his intentions, however, perfection of the heart hasn't yet occurred, and it is more difficult than he thought (*Always pain before a child is born/ Still I'm waiting for the dawn*). Metamorphosis is a slow, painful process. Birth has been described in a similar way. Just as the woman experiences birth pangs during labor, so the Sojourner aches as her heart is broken and made new. The pain and waiting are agonizing. The b-side "Are You Gonna Wait Forever," expresses a continuing prayer for all who journey toward Yahweh. It reiterates the psalmists' ancient prayer, "How long, O Lord? Are you going to wait forever?" *I'm getting closer / we're getting closer to home / It won't be long 'til the summer comes.*[30]

Still there is a longing for Yahweh to come and fulfill his promise (*Are you gonna wait forever?*). Our malaise does not allow us to be content with where we are. We are not satisfied with the state of our world. The gap between rich and poor, healthy and diseased, complacent and committed is too vast. We know justice will be done. We know that Yahweh will one day restore this broken earth, this fragile humanity. But when?

With the knowledge that the journey will soon be over, and the end is in sight, the Sojourner is empowered with a new boldness. There is no more time for hiding (*getting out from under my bed now*). The time for lingering has expired. Words that may have been muffled in the past now need to be spoken with clarity (*gonna say the things I should've said now*). As they are spoken, the Sojourner rediscovers that her identity is interwoven in Christ (*gonna find myself in you*). She connects with the apostle Paul when he writes,

> What actually took place is this: I tried keeping the rules and working my head off to please God, and it didn't work. So I quit being a "law man" so that I could be God's man. Christ's life showed me how, and enabled me to do it. I identified myself completely with him. Indeed, I

---

[30] "Are You Gonna Wait Forever?" from the single *Vertigo*. © 2004 Universal International Music BV.

have been crucified with Christ. My ego is no longer central. It is no longer important that I appear righteous before you or have your good opinion, and I am no longer driven to impress God. Christ lives in me. The life you see me living is not "mine," but it is lived by faith in the Son of God, who loved me and gave himself for me. I am not going to go back on that.[31]

Nor is the Sojourner. There is no going back. Not when Yahweh has offered everything through his Son. We've come too far. And the longer the Sojourner pleads with God, questioning, "Are you going to wait forever," the more clear it becomes that maybe, just maybe, she does not need to wait any longer. Perhaps God isn't waiting forever. Perhaps he has responded to the prayer of "take my heart," and accepted the offer. Due to his acceptance of our identity centered in Christ, he works in and through us, making a difference now.[32] What does God say in response to our prayer, "Don't worry about the little things in life. The furniture can be rearranged. *Don't trade your dreams for some small change.* Guard the flame of your faith, or better, leave it naked and let it spread."[33]

We have traveled a great distance together. From the level, orientated desert plains of *The Joshua Tree,* to wandering under the atomic skies of the disorientated city of *Zooropa,* through the Wilderness of re-orientated

---

[31] Galatians 2:19-21 (The Message).

[32] "By means of his one Spirit, we all say goodbye to our partial and piecemeal lives. We each used to independently call our own shots, but then we entered into a large and integrated life in which *he* has the final say in everything. (This is what we proclaimed in word and action when we were baptized.) Each of us is now a part of his resurrection body, refreshed and sustained at one fountain—his Spirit—where we all come to drink. The old labels we once used to identify ourselves—labels like Jew or Greek, slave or free—are no longer useful. We need something larger, more comprehensive," 1 Corinthians 12:12-13 (The Message).

[33] "Therefore I tell you, do not worry about your life, what you will eat or what you will drink, or about your body, what you will wear. Is not life more than food, and the body more than clothing?" (Matthew 6:25). "You are the light of the world. A city built on a hill cannot be hid. No one after lighting a lamp puts it under the bushel basket, but on the lamp-stand, and it gives light to all in the house. In the same way, let your light shine before others, so that they may see your good works and give glory to your Father in heaven," Matthew 5:14-16.

Vertigo, the road home has been marked with many obstacles. It has been, and continues to be, a long voyage. Yet as each day passes, we are *one step closer to knowing.* We are closer to knowing ourselves, our companions, and ultimately our destination, God himself.[34] We're getting closer to home, to what's true. It won't be much longer until summer arrives with its rich, rewarding harvest. Yahweh, for the sake of us all, may your summer come soon.

---

[34] "One Step Closer," from the album *How to Dismantle an Atomic Bomb.* © 2004 Universal International Music BV.

7
Where Do We Go From Here?[1]

"I need thy sense of future
Teach me to know that life is ever
On the side of the future.
Keep alive in me the forward look, the high hope,
The onward surge. Let me not be frozen
Either by the past or the present."[2]

"Don't trade your dreams for some small change
Guard the flame or better, leave it naked"[3]

Where to now? How is this book applicable to the reader? Well, that depends. It depends on which stream you may belong to. According to my limited math, there are four possible groups to which you, the reader, could belong. They are as follows:

A) You are neither a U2 fan nor a Christ follower.

---

[1] From "With A Shout," from the album *October*. © 1981 Island Records Ltd.
[2] Howard Thurman, *Deep Is the Hunger* (New York: Harper & Row, 1951) 204.
[3] "Are You Gonna Wait Forever," from the single *Vertigo*. © 2004 Universal International Music BV.

B) You are a U2 fan with no real connection to Jesus Christ.

C) You are a Christian with no connection to U2.

D) You are both a U2 fan and a Christ follower.

That should cover all of the categories. Let me add some comments and offer possible suggestions for continuing where you find yourself on the journey of faith and popular culture.

Let's begin with group A. What can I write except, if you have actually made it this far through the book, perhaps faith in God has intrigued you. Perhaps during this reading you may have borrowed one or two U2 CDs from your local library or purchased a few songs from iTunes. I would encourage you to continue listening to what the songs are saying, and even go so far as to pick up a Bible to see what it has to say about life and faith.

Moving to group B, I love your enthusiasm and share your excitement for all things U2. Needless to say, there are many fans out there who appreciate the minutia of every U2 song, picking up on the smallest of details (especially all the fans at atU2.com). I would urge you to pay close attention and listen. As excellent as U2's songs are musically, their lyrical undercurrents flow at great depths and offer much spiritual and theological fodder. To enhance your reflection, I would recommend three books. If you haven't already, read *Walk On: The Spiritual Journey of U2* by Steve Stockman and *Get Up Off Your Knees: Preaching the U2 Catalog* edited by Raewynne J. Whiteley and Beth Maynard. The former offers a primer on matters U2 and spirituality while the latter is a collection of sermons either involving or based on U2 lyrics. The third book is one on the top of Bono's reads. It is *The Message*, a fresh and dynamic version of the Bible translated by Eugene Peterson.

For those who find themselves within group C, perhaps this book has been read out of sheer curiosity as to how God could possibly speak through a rock and roll band. I believe that in order to be able to communicate the gospel effectively, one must be aware of, and have an understanding of, the surrounding culture. After reading this book, I would hope that you "listen prayerfully to the world around you."[4] At the time of this publication, U2 is the largest, most popular, and best (as U2 themselves

---

[4] Whiteley and Maynard, *Get Up Off Your Knees: Preaching the U2 Catalog*, 164.

claim) ticket on the planet. What I have previously called the U2 phenomenon still holds true. This band, through their music and activist message, are shaping culture, society, and the political landscape on a global scale. Hopefully, this book will have revealed the reality that there is a conversation of faith taking place outside the four walls of your church, your social gatherings, your youth groups, your idea of Christendom. If you are willing to step beyond the safety of a sterile, self-constructed Christianity, the discussion of faith is open, waiting for you to take your seat. People are eager to hear what you have to share. Are you listening prayerfully to the world around you? Are you willing to prayerfully participate in the dialogue of faith with those around you thirsting for something real?

Lastly, welcome to my place. I think it safe to write that I have an appreciation for this band called U2. Those who know me have undoubtedly said, if not thought, that I should pursue nobler, more serious endeavors, other than listening to, watching, reading, and writing about U2. What they don't realize, however, is how much fun this is. Perhaps you have experienced something similar. Interestingly enough, another group of people wonder why we waste our efforts "listening" to, reading about, and praying to Jesus Christ. How primitive in such an advanced world. What they don't realize, however, is how life-changing this is. Herein lies the difference between being an ardent U2 fan and a devoted follower of Christ. One is life-enhancing while the other is life-transforming. One involves happiness and pleasure, the other joy and peace. It is true, U2's music and lyrics stimulate my faith, and in turn my faith provides me with a deeper appreciation of the songs' nuances.

For the readers who take part in my world, keep establishing links between this present world and the one that is to come. Keep making connections between the now and the not yet. Keep building bridges across the vast chasms that separate the Church and her surrounding neighborhood. Keep on keeping the faith. Keep on sharing the faith. And if that means using the "life-enhancing" to offer the "life-transforming," then don't just guard the flame, better yet, leave it naked.

Recommended Listening

Track 1 - "Drowning Man" © 1983 Island Records Ltd. Words and music by U2. From the album *War*.

Track 2 - "Until the End of the World" © 1991 Island Records Ltd. Words and music by U2. From the album *Achtung Baby*.

Track 3 - "New Year's Day" © 1983 Island Records Ltd. Words and music by U2. From the album *War*.

Track 4 - "Bullet the Blue Sky (Live)" © 1993 Island Records Inc. Words by Bono, music by U2. From the single *Stay (Faraway, So Close!)*.

Track 5 - "Mothers of the Disappeared" © 1987 Island Records Ltd. Words by Bono, music by U2. From the album *The Joshua Tree*.

Track 6 - "Where the Streets Have No Name" © 2001 Universal Music International BV. Words and music by U2. From the single *Walk On*.

Track 7 - "I Still Haven't Found What I'm Looking For" © 1988 Island Records Ltd. Words by Bono, music by U2. From the album *Rattle and Hum*.

Track 8 - "Love Is Blindness" © 1991 Island Records Ltd. Words and music by U2. From the album *Achtung Baby*.

Track 9 - "Zooropa" © 1993 Polygram International Music BV. Words by Bono, music by U2. From the album *Zooropa*.

Track 10 - "Lemon" © 1993 Polygram International Music BV. Words by Bono, music by U2. From the album *Zooropa*.

Track 11 - "The Wanderer" © 1993 Polygram International Music BV. Words by Bono, music by U2. From the album *Zooropa* (sung by Johnny Cash).

Track 12 - "Playboy Mansion" © 1997 Polygram International Music BV. Words by Bono and The Edge, music by U2. From the album *Pop*.

Track 13 - "Wake up Dead Man" © 1997 Polygram International Music BV. Words by Bono and The Edge, music by U2. From the album *Pop*.

Track 14 - "Beautiful Day" © 2000 Universal International Music BV. Words by Bono, music by U2. From the album *All That You Can't Leave Behind*.

Track 15 - "Walk On" © 2000 Universal International Music BV. Words by Bono, music by U2. From the album *All That You Can't Leave Behind*.

Track 16 - "Always" © 2000 Universal International Music BV. Words by Bono, music by U2. From the single *Beautiful Day*.

Recommended Listening

Track 17 - "Vertigo" © 2004 Universal International Music BV. Words by Bono with The Edge, music by U2. From the album *How To Dismantle An Atomic Bomb*.

Track 18 - "Falling At Your Feet" © 2000 Universal Island Records Ltd. Words and music by Bono and Daniel Lanois. From the soundtrack *The Million Dollar Hotel*.

Track 19 - "Love and Peace or Else" © 2004 Universal International Music BV. Words by Bono with The Edge, music by U2. From the album *How To Dismantle An Atomic Bomb*.

Track 20 - "Yahweh" © 2004 Universal International Music BV. Words by Bono with The Edge, music by U2. From the album *How To Dismantle An Atomic Bomb*.

Track 21 - "Do You Feel Loved" © 1997 Polygram International Music BV. Words by Bono and The Edge, music by U2. From the album *Pop*.

Track 22 - "Are You Gonna Wait Forever?" © 2004 Universal International Music BV. Words by Bono, music by U2. From the single *Vertigo*.

U2 Inspired Litany

Inspired by Mark 15 and various U2 lyrics, the following litany was written by Robert Vagacs, and edited by Brian Walsh for "Wine Before Breakfast," a Tuesday morning Eucharist service hosted at Wycliffe College, University of Toronto. This prayer was read in community on March 26, 2002.

LET US PRAY:

Lord Jesus,
Truly you are the King of the Jews,
you are the King of every race.
Forgive us for choosing hatred and violence,
murder and insurrection, over your Way of
love, peace, life, and humility.
Forgive us for choosing Barabbas over you.
We fall at your feet and pray for forgiveness.

Every chip from every cup
Every promise given up

A U2 Inspired Litany

Every reason that's not enough
Is falling, falling at your feet[1]

We thank you for the father of Alexander and Rufus,
for Simon the passer-by who for a moment shared your burden.
Thank you for the gift of our friends and family.
Thank you for the gift of this community,
which gathers in your name on Tuesday mornings.
Thank you for every divinely appointed "passer-by"
who has crossed our path of peril to offer some support.
Thank you. Thank you. Thank you.

Everyone who needs a friend
Every life that has no end
Every knee not ready to bend
Is falling, falling at your feet
We've come crawling, now we're falling at your feet [2]

Lord Jesus,
Truly you are the Son of God.
Your night ran over and your day did not last,
and you gave yourself away.[3]

Thank you for choosing obedience and trust.
Thank you for choosing pain and rejection.
Thank you for choosing death and sacrifice.
Thank you for choosing us.

We live in an aching world that is compassless,
that has no map, no particular place names, no particular song.[4]

---

[1] "Falling at Your Feet," from the soundtrack *The Million Dollar Hotel.* © 2000 Universal Island Records Ltd.

[2] Ibid.

[3] From the songs, "Stuck In A Moment You Can't Get Out Of," from the album *All That You Can't Leave Behind.* © 2000 Universal International Music BV, and "With Or Without You," from the album *The Joshua Tree.* © 1987 Island Records Ltd.

[4] "Zooropa," from the album *Zooropa.* © 1993 Polygram International Music BV.

When you look at the world
what is it that you see?
People find all kinds of things
that bring them to their knees.[5]
Yet a day will come
when every knee will bow and every tongue confess
you as Lord.

Then will there be no time of sorrow.
Then will there be no time for pain.
Then will there be no time of sorrow.
Then will there be no time for shame.[6]

Yet now is a time filled with sorrow.
Now is a time of pain.
Now is a time of confusion.
For the many who suffer in body, mind, and soul,
we pray:

Comfort! Restore! Heal! Remember!
Remember those whom you have chosen.
Remember those whose names
you have inscribed on the palms of your hands.[7]

(a moment for silent or spoken prayers for those in need)

They are the bandits on your left and right.
They are the ones hurling insults.
They are the soldiers just taking orders.
They are the politicians making compromises.
They are the widows at your feet.
They are your disciples, scattered like sheep, nowhere to be found.

---

[5] "When I Look At The World," from the album *All That You Can't Leave Behind.* ©
2000 Universal International Music BV.
[6] "Playboy Mansion," from the album *Zooropa.* © 1997 Polygram International Music
BV.
[7] Isaiah 49:16.

A U2 Inspired Litany

I was there when they crucified my Lord,
I held the scabbard as the soldier drew his sword,
I threw the dice when they pierced his side,
But I've seen love conquer the great divide.[8]

Worthy is the Lamb that was
slaughtered,

to receive power and wealth and
    wisdom and might
and honor and glory and
    blessing![9]

Amen.

---

[8] "When Love Comes To Town," from the album *Rattle and Hum*. © 1988 Island Records
Ltd.
[9] Revelation 5:12.

U2 Discography

Boy, Island Records, 1980. Produced by Steve Lillywhite.

October, Island Records, 1981. Produced by Steve Lillywhite.

War, Island Records, 1983. Produced by Steve Lillywhite.

Under a Blood Red Sky, Island Records, 1983. Produced by Jimmy Iovine.

The Unforgettable Fire, Island Records, 1984. Produced by Brian Eno and Daniel Lanois.

The Joshua Tree, Island Records, 1987. Produced by Daniel Lanois and Brian Eno.

Rattle and Hum, Island Records, 1988. Produced by Jimmy Iovine.

Achtung Baby, Island Records, 1991. Produced by Daniel Lanois and Brian Eno.

Zooropa, Island Records, 1993. Produced by Flood, Brian Eno, and The Edge.

Passengers: Original Soundtracks 1, Island/Polygram Records, 1995.

Pop, Island/Polygram Records, 1997. Produced by Flood.

U2 Discography

U2: The Best of 1980–1990, Island/Polygram Records, 1998.

All That You Can't Leave Behind, Universal Island Records, 2000. Produced by Daniel Lanois and Brian Eno.

U2: The Best of 1990–2000, Universal Music International BV, 2002.

How to Dismantle an Atomic Bomb, Universal Music International BV, 2004. Produced by Steve Lillywhite.

Sources

America: A Tribute to Heroes. Produced by Joel Gallen. 120 min. Warner Bros., Universal, Sony, BMG, EMI, 2001. DVD.

Anderson, Ray S. *The Gospel According to Judas: Is There a Limit to God's Forgiveness?* Colorado Springs: NavPress, 1994.

Anderson, Walter Truett, ed. *The Truth About the Truth: De-confusing and Re-constructing the Postmodern World.* New York: Tarcher/Putnam, 1995.

Assayas, Michka. *Bono in Conversation with Michka Assayas.* New York: Riverhead Books, 2005.

Averill, Steve, and Shaughn McGrath. *Stealing Hearts at a Travelling Show: The Graphic Design of U2 by FOUR5ONECREATIVE.* Dublin: FOUR5ONECREATIVE, 2003.

Bauckman, Richard, and Trevor Hart. *Hope Against Hope: Christian Eschatology at the Turn of the Millennium.* Grand Rapids: Eerdmans, 1999.

Beeaff, Diane Ebertt. *A Grand Madness: Ten Years on the Road with U2.* Arizona: Hawkmoon, 2000.

Blow, Richard. "Bono Turns Up the Political Heat." *George Magazine,* April 2000, 62.

Bono (Paul Hewson). Interview by Claire Cibik. *CNN People in the News: Bono,* www.cnn.com.

Brueggemann, Walter. *The Message of the Psalms: A Theological Commentary.* Minneapolis: Augsburg, 1984.

———. *David's Truth in Israel's Imagination and Memory.* Minneapolis: Fortress Press, 1985.

———. *The Hopeful Imagination: Prophetic Voices in Exile.* Philadelphia: Fortress Press, 1986.

Sources

_____. *Israel's Praise: Doxology against Idolatry and Ideology.* Philadelphia: Fortress Press, 1988.

_____. *Finally Comes the Poet: Daring Speech for Proclamation.* Minneapolis: Fortress Press, 1989.

_____. *Abiding Astonishment: Psalms, Modernity, and the Making of History.* Louisville: WJK Press, 1991.

_____. *A Social Reading of the Old Testament: Prophetic Approaches to Israel's Communal Life.* Minneapolis: Fortress Press, 1994.

_____. *The Psalms and the Life of Faith.* Minneapolis: Fortress Press, 1995.

_____. *Cadences of Home: Preaching Among Exiles.* Louisville, Kentucky: WJK Press, 1997.

_____. *A Commentary on Jeremiah: Exile and Homecoming.* Grand Rapids: Eerdmans, 1998.

_____. *The Prophetic Imagination,* 2d ed. Minneapolis: Fortress Press, 2001.

Capps, Walter Holden. *Hope Against Hope: Moltmann to Merton in One Theological Decade.* Philadelphia: Fortress Press, 1976.

Corbijn, Anton. *U2 & I: The Photographs 1982–2004.* Verona: Schirmer/Mosel, 2005.

Crossan, John Dominic. *The Dark Interval: Toward a Theology of Story.* Niles, Illinois: Argus, 1975.

Deevoy, Adrian. "U2 Walk On Water!" *Blender,* November 2004, 112.

Dunphy, Eamon. *Unforgettable Fire: Past, Present, and Future—The Definitive Biography of U2.* New York: Warner, 1987.

Eccleston, Danny, ed. *U2: Elevation U2001 Tour Programme.* 2001.

Elliott, Michael. "Right Man, Right Time." *Time Magazine,* March 4, 2002, 68.

Ellul, Jacques. *Hope in Time of Abandonment.* Translated by C. Edward Hopkin. New York: Seabury Press, 1973.

Essex, Andrew. "Unforgettable Fire." *Details Magazine,* November 2001, 120–27.

Fiddes, Paul S. *The Promised End: Eschatology in Theology and Literature.* Oxford: Blackwell, 2000.

Flanagan, Bill. *U2 at the End of the World.* New York: Delacorte Press, 1995.

Fricke, David. "U2 Drops Bomb." *Rolling Stone,* December 2004–January 2005, 56.

Gergen, Kenneth J. *The Saturated Self: Dilemmas of Identity in Contemporary Life.* New York: Basic Books, 1991.

Goldmann, Lucien. *The Hidden God: A Study of Tragic Vision in the "Pensées" of Pascal and the Tragedies of Racine.* Translated by Philip Thody. New York: Humanities Press, 1964.

Goudzwaard, Bob. *Idols of Our Time.* Translated by Mark Vander Vennen. Iowa: Dordt College Press, 1984.

Grenz, Stanley J. *A Primer On Postmodernism.* Grand Rapids: Eerdmans, 1996.

Grenz, Stanley J., and John R. Franke. *Beyond Foundationalism: Shaping Theology in a Postmodern Context.* Louisville: WJK Press, 2001.

Heath, Chris. "U2: Band of the Year." *Rolling Stone Magazine,* January 18, 2001, 36.

_____. "U2 Tour: From the Heart." *Rolling Stone Magazine,* 10 May 2001.

Klosterman, Chuck. "Mysterious Days." *Spin,* December 2004, 58.

Lakeland, Paul. *Postmodernity: Christian Identity in a Fragmented Age.* Minneapolis: Fortress Press, 1997.

Lasor, William Sanford, David Allan Hubbard, and Frederic Wm. Bush. *Old Testament Survey: The Message, Form, and Background of the Old Testament,* 2d ed. Grand Rapids: Eerdmans, 1996.

Light, Alan. "Band of the Year: Rock's Unbreakable Heart." *Spin Magazine,* January 2002, 56–62.

Lynch, William F. *Images of Hope: Imagination as Healer of the Hopeless.* Dublin: Helicon, 1965.

Maddex, Bobby. "A God-Shaped Hole: Can U2 and a New Generation of Seekers Ever Fill It?" *Gadfly,* August 1997, 4.

Middleton, J. Richard, and Brian J. Walsh. *Truth is Stranger Than it Used to Be: Biblical Faith in a Postmodern Age.* Downers Grove: InterVarsity Press, 1995.

_____. "Theology at the 'Rim of a Broken Wheel': Bruce Cockburn and Christian Faith in a Postmodern World." *Grail: An Ecumenical Journal* (June 1993): 14–39.

Moltmann, Jürgen. *Experiences of God.* Translated by Margaret Kohl. London: SCM Press Ltd., 1980.

Mueller, Andrew, ed. *U2 Vertigo 2005 Tour Programme.* 2005.

Newbigin, Lesslie. *The Gospel in a Pluralist Society.* Grand Rapids: Eerdmans/WCC, 1989.

Osborn, Bud. *Hundred Block Rock.* Vancouver: Arsenal Pulp Press, 1999.

Parra (de la), Pimm Jal. *U2 Live: A Concert Documentary.* New York: Omnibus Press, 1997.

Philbrook, Erik. "Keeping the Peace." *Playback,* October 2001, www.ascap.com.

Postman, Neil. *Amusing Ourselves to Death: Public Discourse in the Age of Show Business.* New York: Penguin, 1985.

Rees, Paul. "Riders On The Storm." *Q,* November 2004, 68.

Review of *U2's Elevation Tour Concert at the United Center, Chicago,* by Greg Kot. *Chicago Metromix,* 18 October 2001, www.metromix.com.

Selections from the Book of Psalms. With an introduction by Bono. New York: Grove Press, 1999.

Scrimgeour, Diana. *U2 Show.* London: Orion, 2004.

Sittler, Joseph. *Evocations of Grace: Writings on Ecology, Theology, and Ethics.* Grand Rapids: Eerdmans, 2000.

Smith, James K.A. *The Fall of Interpretation: Philosophical Foundations for a Creational Hermeneutic.* Downers Grove: IVP, 2000.

Stockman, Steve. *Walk On: The Spiritual Journey of U2.* Florida: Relevant Books, 2001.

Stokes, Niall, ed. *The U2 File: A Hot Press U2 History.* Dublin: Hot Press, 1985.

_____. *Into the Heart: The Stories Behind Every U2 Song.* Dubai: Carlton, 1996.

The Million Dollar Hotel. Produced by Deepak Nayar, Bono, Nicholas Klein, Bruce Davey, and Wim Wenders. 122 min. Alliance Atlantis, 2000. DVD.

Sources

Turner, Steve. *Hungry for Heaven: Rock 'n' Roll & the Search for Redemption*. Downers Grove, Illinois: IVP, 1995.

Tyrangiel, Josh. "Rock the Power: Bono." *Time Magazine*, March 4, 2002, 60–70.

U2: The Rolling Stone Files. New York: Rolling Stone Press, 1994.

U2. *Achtung Baby: the Videos, the Cameos and a Whole Lot of Interference* From Zoo TV. Produced by Ned O'Hanlon and directed by Maurice Linnane. 25.46 min. Island/Polygram, 1991. Videocassette.

_____. *Elevation 2001/U2 Live from Boston*. Produced by Ned O'Hanlon and directed by Hamish Hamilton. Universal, 2001. DVD.

_____. *Talk Pop*. Interview by Dave Fanning. Island, 1997. CD.

_____. *U2: Popmart Live from Mexico City*. Produced by Ned O'Hanlon and directed by David Mallet. 2 hrs, 7 min. Island/Polygram, 1998. Videocassette.

_____. *U2: The Joshua Tree*. Produced by Chips Chipperfield and directed by Philip King and Nuala O'Connor. Eagle Rock Entertainment, 1999. DVD.

_____. *U2: Rattle and Hum*. Produced by Michael Hamlyn and directed by Phil Joanou. 98 min. Paramount, 1988. DVD.

_____. *U2: Zoo TV Live from Sydney*. Produced by Ned O'Hanlon and directed by David Mallet. 1 hr, 58 min. Island/Polygram, 1994. Videocassette.

_____. *Walk On*. Produced by Daniel Lanois and Brian Eno and directed by Jonas Akerlund. Universal, 2001. DVD.

VanderSpek, Henry. *Faith, Hope & U2: The Spirit of Love in U2's Music*. Richmond, BC: InterVarsity Press, 2000.

Vanhoozer, Kevin J., ed. *The Cambridge Companion to Postmodern Theology*. Cambridge: Cambridge, 2003.

Walsh, Brian J., and J. Richard Middleton. *The Transforming Vision: Shaping a Christian World View*. Downers Grove: InterVarsity Press, 1984.

Walsh, Brian J. "The Christian Worldview of Bruce Cockburn: Prophetic Art in a Dangerous Time." *Toronto Journal of Theology* (Fall 1989): 170–87.

_____. *Subversive Christianity: Imaging God in a Dangerous Time*. Seattle: Alta Vista College Press, 1994.

Whiteley, Raewynne J., and Beth Maynard, eds. *Get Up Off Your Knees: Preaching the U2 Catalog*. Cambridge: Cowley, 2003.

Willman, Chris. "Arch Deluxe." *Entertainment Weekly*, May 9, 1997, 30–37.

Wolterstorff, Nicholas. *Until Justice and Peace Embrace*. Grand Rapids: Eerdmans, 1983.